Frank Hamilton Fowler

The Negatives of the Indo-European Languages

Frank Hamilton Fowler

The Negatives of the Indo-European Languages

ISBN/EAN: 9783743394926

Manufactured in Europe, USA, Canada, Australia, Japa

Cover: Foto ©Paul-Georg Meister /pixelio.de

Manufactured and distributed by brebook publishing software
(www.brebook.com)

Frank Hamilton Fowler

The Negatives of the Indo-European Languages

THE NEGATIVES

OF THE

INDO-EUROPEAN LANGUAGES

A DISSERTATION PRESENTED TO THE FACULTY OF
ARTS, LITERATURE, AND SCIENCE, OF THE
UNIVERSITY OF CHICAGO, IN CANDIDACY
FOR THE DEGREE OF DOCTOR
OF PHILOSOPHY

BY
FRANK HAMILTON FOWLER

The University of Chicago Press
1896

THE NEGATIVES OF THE INDO-EUROPEAN LANGUAGES.

PRIMITIVE INDO-EUROPEAN.

I. I.E. *mē:* Skr. *mā*, Av. *mā*, O.P. *mā*, Gr. μή (Doric μή), Arm. *mi*, Alb. *mo-* (in *mo-s*).

II. I.E. *ne:* Skr. *na*, Goth. *ni*, Lith. *nè*, O.B. *ne*, Lat. *ne*, Osc. *ne*, Umbr. *ne*. I.E. *nē:* Skr. *nā*, Lat. *nē*, Osc. *ni*, Goth. *nē*, O.Ir. *nī*. I.E. *nō:* Lat. *nōn*, Umbr. *no-* (in *no-sve*), O.Ir. *na nā*. The Skr. words given under *ne* and *nē* and various compounds in the Iranian languages may, of course, be connected with either *nē* or *nō*, or with both.

III. I.E. *nei:* Av. *naē-* (in *naē-ciš, naē-da*), Lith. *nei nè-*, Lat. *nei nī*, Osc. *nei*, Umbr. *nei-* (in *nei-p*), probably also in O.P. *naiy.* I.E. *noi:* Lat. *noe-* (in *noe-num* and in Duenos *noi-si* and *noi-ne* (?)), Lith. *nai-* (in *nai-kinu*). As in the case of I.E. *nē* and *nō*, forms in Aryan from I.E. *nei* and *noi* cannot be distinguished.

IV. I.E. *ṇ:* Skr. *a- an-*, Av. *a- an-*, O.P. *a*, Arm. *an-*, Gr. ἀ- ἀν-, Lat. *in-*, O.Ir. *an-*, Germanic *un-*. I.E. *ṇ̄:* Gr. νη- (Dor. νᾱ-), Osc. *an-*, Umbr. *an-*, O.H.G. *ā-*, O.E. *ē-*.

Of these I.E. negatives, without doubt *nei* and *noi* are *ne* and *no* strengthened by the particle *i̯*, seen in various places elsewhere.[1] I.E. *nei* and *noi*, then, are examples of a phenomenon — the strengthening of a negative — which was often repeated in the separate developments.

The relation of *ne nē no nō* is plainly one of ablaut; and it would seem most natural to consider *ṇ ṇ̄* as the weak ablaut forms of the same particle.[2] The prevailing use of *ṇ ṇ̄* in the separate languages as negative prefixes indicates that those forms were in the proethnic speech the negatives of nouns. Now it is easy to

---

[1] *E. g.*, in pronouns (Lat. *quoi quī*), in the Locative suffixes singular and plural (-*i*, *s-i* beside *s-u*); probably also the same particle differentiates the primary from the secondary verb endings. *Cf.* Brugmann, II, 414, 424, 256, 356, 909 ; O. Brugmann, Ni., 32 ; Per Persson, I.F., 2, 247 ; Thurneysen, K.Z., 27, 177.

[2] So Schulze, K.Z., 27, 606, and others.

understand that there should be differences between the prevailing accentual relations in combinations of negative and verb and of negative and noun which should give rise to different ablaut forms of the negative particle. According to Delbrück[1] this difference is to be connected with the enclisis of the verb in independent sentences. But Zimmer[2] has argued conclusively, I think, that the condition of verbal enclisis in I.E. was not position in an independent sentence, but was simply a matter of sentence accent. It would still be the case, however, that in a collocation of negative and verb the verb would generally be enclitic, and the result of this is clearly shown in the conditions of verbal enclisis in O.Ir. The only objection to considering the various negative prefixes mentioned above as representatives of I.E. η and $\bar{\eta}$ and these as weak ablaut forms of ne is the presence of such dissyllabic forms as Av. ana-, Gr. $\dot{a}\nu a$-. But these, I think, are to be disposed of otherwise (see p. 8).

The forms η $\bar{\eta}$ were the *only* ones used with nouns in the proethnic speech. With the exception of the Balto-Slavic, none of the languages has *ne*, *nē*, *no*, or *nō* used as a negative prefix.[3] The common occurrence of compounds of a negative with an *indefinite* adverb or pronoun (*e. g.*, Skr. *ná-kis*, *mā́-kis;* Av. *naē-cīš;* Gr. μή-τις, μή-πω, μη-δείς, οὐδείς ; Lat. *nēmo*, *nun-quam*, *nē-cubi;* Eng. *none*, *never*, etc.) is no evidence for the use as a prefix of the negative so compounded.[4] A sharp distinction is to be made between such compounds and compounds like ἄνιππος, *intactus*, *unhappy*, etc. With these *indefinite* compounds the *negative prefixes* of a given language never occur. This is seen most clearly in Balto-Slavic.[5] In other languages representatives of I.E. *ne* may appear compounded with indefinites, but here where alone I.E. *ne* becomes a negative prefix it is not so used. The *indefinite* compound arises from collocation in the sentence. In a sentence containing a

[1] Syn. Forsch., IV, 146.

[2] Festgruss an Roth, 173; *cf.* Hirt, Akzent, 304 f.

[3] The very few words in other languages which have sometimes been mentioned as showing *ne*- used as negative prefix I shall speak of under the several languages.

[4] Hirt (Akzent, 312 f.) has most recently fallen into this error of citing indefinite compounds in support of the supposition that the form *ne* was used as a prefix.

[5] *Cf.* Lith. *nevěns*, "non unus sed plures," and *nei věns*, "nullus;" and see Gebauer. Archiv f. Slav. Phil., 8, 177 ff.

sentence-negative and in which the verb has for its subject an
indefinite pronoun or is modified by an indefinite adverb the
effect is the same whether the negative is felt with the verb or
with the indefinite subject or adverb. The same is not true if
the subject, for example, is other than indefinite.[1]

So far as I know, the only alleged example of a proethnic
noun showing *ne-* as a negative prefix is *nepot-* (Skr. *napāt,* Gr.
νέποδες, Lat. *nepōs,* etc.[2]), regarded by many as a compound of *ne*
and *pot-* (Skr. *pati-,* Gr. πόσις, Lat. *potis,* Goth. *fadi*). But the iso-
lation of the word in this respect should make us skeptical of an
etymology, which, moreover, on its semasiological side is none
too convincing.[3]

I prefer to start with a root *nep-*[4], with meaning "to bring
forth" or something of the sort, to which was added a suffix
consisting of a dental preceded by a vowel. With this root is
to be connected the root *neb-,* in Gr. νεβρός, which I shall have
occasion to discuss below.

As for the suffix *-od* or *-ot,* which we have to assume if we take
the root to be *nep-,* we may suppose that the suffix was *-od,* and
that the *-d-* stem became a *-t-* stem owing to the scarcity of the
-d- stems, except in Greek where *-d-* stems were more numerous.[5]

[1] Three other classes of compounds in which negatives occur might be
mentioned, *viz.,* strengthened negative adverbs, *e. g.,* I.E. *nei̯ noi̯,* Skr. *na-nú.*
Gr. οὐ-κί, etc.; compounds in which for the most part the original force of the
two elements is retained, *e. g.,* Lat. *neque,* Goth. *ni-h;* compounds which are
in origin elliptical expressions, *e. g.,* Lat. *nīmīrum,* Skr. *nǻsti-ka.*

[2] *Cf.* Prellwitz, *sub v.* νέποδες; Osthoff, Perfect., 599; J. Baunack, Studien,
272; Leumann, Festgruss an Böthlingk, 77; Streitberg, I.F., III, 334; de Saussure, Mem. Soc. Ling., III, 196; Brugmann, II, 123; and see Panini, V, 3, 75,
for the origin of the derivation.

[3] Skr. *napā́t napt̥r* Grassmann defines as 1) Abkömmling, 2) Sohn, 3) Enkel;
the Av. *napat* means "descendant," Av. *napti* "posterity;" O.B. *netiji̯* "Ge
schwistersohn;" Bohemian *neti* "niece;" O.II.G. *nefo* "grandson," "relative;"
Lat. *nepōs* "descendant," "nephew," "grandson;" Lat. *neptis* "granddaugh-
ter;" Gr. νέποδες "children;" Gr. ἀνεψιός "nephew" (see Prellwitz *sub v.*).
The meanings of the words in the various languages ("nephew," "grandson,"
"descendant") indicate that at the end of the I.E. period the word had the
meaning "descendant." The usual etymology leads to the meaning "weakling." The supposition that the idea of "descendant" was derived from that
of "weakling" is, of course, possible, but hardly satisfactory.

[4] *Cf.* Spiegel, K.Z., 14, 392.

[5] *Cf.* Brugmann, I, 128; Osthoff, Perfect., 159. The presence of πώς in
Greek might exert an especial influence in keeping the *-d-*.

The suffixal -*d*-, though never very common — except in Greek —, is found after various vowels[1]: -*ad*, Gr. φυγ-αδ-; -*id*- (probably I.E. in some cases), Gr. ἀσπ-ιδ-, Lat. *capid;* -*ud*, Lat. *pal-ūd-;* *ud*, Lat. *pec-ud-;* *ed* or *ed*, Lat. *her-ed-*. A suffix -*od*- would not be strange, though unsupported by more than this one example. It is to be noted, however, that three or four words in Sanskrit — *dṛṣád* "rock," *bhasád* "back parts," *çarad* "autumn," and *vanád*(?) "desire" — may have I.E. -*od*, and that the Germanic words with -*at-* — *e. g.,* Goth. *lauh-at-jan,* O.H.G. *lohazzen* — speak as much for I.E. *od* as -*ad*-, unless indeed -*at-jan* is to be taken as equivalent to Gr. -αζειν. To be mentioned in the same connection is the common Goth. and West Germanic suffix -*assus*.[2]

Or, on the other hand, the suffix may be an example of the class, limited in number, of suffixes consisting of -*t*- preceded by a vowel, *e. g.,* Skr. *sravát-, marut;* Gr. κέλης, κέλ-ητ-ος; Lat. *teges, seges, caput (*cap-ot);* Osc. liímitú[m]; O.Ir. *cing-*, gen. *cinged;* Goth. *mitaps;* O.H.G. *helid*.[3] In this case we must suppose that the -*t*- was changed to -δ- in Greek under the influence of the -δ- stems, as Osthoff has claimed.

THE NEGATIVES IN THE SEPARATE LANGUAGES.

SANSKRIT.

Skr. *mā*, I.E. *mē*.

The simple negative was strengthened by various particles — *kīm, ū, sma*—, the *mā* keeping its distinctive meaning. With -*kis* it formed *mā-kis*, "nequis."

Skr. *na*, I.E. *ne*.

Skr. *nā*,[4] I.E. *nē*.

Skr. *nēd* is a compound of *na* and *id* (as *cēd* from *ca + id*), the latter undoubtedly a particle from the pronominal stem *i*-seen in Cyprian ἴν (Hesychius), O.Lat. *im*, and in the deictive

[1] Brugmann, II, 123.

[2] *Cf.* Brugmann, II, 108; Bahder, Verbalabstracta, 119.

[3] *Cf.* Brugmann, II, 123, for other examples, and Walter, K.Z., X, 194 ff., in regard to Latin *eques, miles,* etc. It can hardly be that these words are compounds of -*i-t-*, "going," and even in case of *com-es* and *anti-stes* the supposition is doubtful. *Cf.* Wharton, s. v. *comes*. See also de Saussure, Mem. Soc. Ling., III, 197.

[4] *E. g.,* R.V., 10, 348.

particle *ī* mentioned above under I.E. *nei*. The compound was Aryan (*naid*, Av. *nōiṯ*). Skr. *na-kĭm*, *na-hi*, *na-nú* show *na* strengthened by various particles.

Skr. *na* was not used as a prefix. Of Panini's list[1] *napāt* has been considered above. The rest are either altogether fanciful, as *nakula*, "ichneumon," or manifestly impossible, as *navedas*, "knowing," with the exception of *napuṅsaka*, "hermaphrodite." But I hardly think the word can stand alone as an example of the use of *na-* as a prefix. The *na-* is probably the same as that seen in *na-vedas*, whatever that may be, and the quasi-negative force comes from the diminutive.

In regard to the relation of *na* comparative and *na* negative in Sanskrit, taking into consideration the existence of similar pairs in Balto-Slavic and O.Ir., we should say, I think, that, either in proethnic times or in the separate languages, the comparative was developed from the negative.[2] *Cf.* dialectic English "better nor that."

Skr. *caná* also has generally been taken as a compound of *na* negative.[3] But Per Persson is surely right here in supposing that the negative meaning is a derived one. Whatever the order of development of meaning of *caná*, the uses may be classified as follows :

(*a*) Intensive : 1) In positive sentences, "indeed," 2) with a negative, "(not) indeed."

(*b*) Negative : 1) Strong negative, "indeed not," 2) conjunctional negative, "also not," "and not."

Manifestly three explanations are possible : 1) That *caná*, a compound of *ca* and *na*, negative, was used, first as a negative, then as a second negative intensifying the first, and lastly from being a negative intensifier *caná* came to be an intensifier that could be used in a positive sentence. 2) An explanation, the direct opposite of this, that *caná*, a compound of *ca* and *na* intensive, was used first as an intensive particle and especially to intensify a negative, and finally as an adverb with a negative force

[1] Panini's list (6, 3, 75) is *nabhrāj, napāt, nāsatyā, namuci, nakula, nakha, napuṅsaka, nakṣatra, nakra, navedas,* and *nākā.*

[2] *Cf.* B. and R., *sub v.;* Grassmann, *sub v.;* Delbrück, Syn. Forsch., 5, 543; Pott, Ety. Forsch., 1, 352; and Per Persson, I.F., II, 203.

[3] Grassmann, *sub v.;* Eva Channing, J.A.O.S., 13, XCIX ; Delbrück, Syn. Forsch., V, 544; Per Persson, I.F., 2, 204; and *cf.* Brugmann, II, 421.

of its own. 3) That *caná* intensive and *caná* negative were of different origin.

The very frequent use of *caná* to intensify a negative (in R.V. 57 out of 86, in A.V. all of the 39 cases) would indicate some sort of a connection between the negative and intensive forces of the word. Against the first explanation it is to be said that a composition of *ca* and *na* negative in the order *ca-na* is hardly to be expected; and again, it is difficult to see how *caná* used as a quasi-intensive particle with a negative, with the meaning "(not) .... indeed not"—supposing it to have had that meaning originally—could acquire a purely intensive (positive) force, without being used as a true negative expressing with the preceding negative a simple strong negation. But a collocation of two negatives in the sense of one probably does not occur in Sanskrit,[1] and in fact a "not — not," such as this would be, is impossible anywhere.[2]

[1] Delbrück, Syn. Forsch., V, 544 ; Eva Channing, J.A.O.S., 13, XCIX.

[2] A distinction is to be made between collocations of true negatives with the meaning of one and those which historically are collocations of negative and intensive, the intensive having acquired a negative force. True double negatives are separated in their application. In general one negatives the sentence, while the other is felt with an important word. The most common case is that in which a second negative is used to negative an indefinite pronoun or adverb, *e. g., No one shan't do it; Non miseret neminis*, Enn. Erecth., frag. 4; *Jura te nociturum non esse homini de hac re nemini*, Plaut, Mil, 1411; τά γ' οὐ κέ τις οὐδὲ ἴδοιτο, Od., 8, 280. Very often the negative and the indefinite form a compound. But a negative may be felt to belong to any important word and so two negatives be admitted, *e. g.*, O.E., *Ther nys no table; Neque nucleis ad oleam ne utatur*, Cato, R.R., 66. The need felt for a second negative may be increased if one of the negatives is a conjunction, if the negative is compounded with a verb, or if a number of words intervenes between the first negative and some important word. But these causes act indirectly, and the second negative is still felt with some important word. Of a different sort are double negatives arising from syntactical contamination, *e. g., Forbade the boy he should not pass those grounds*, Shaks., Passionate Pilgrim. For other examples of contamination *cf.* Strong, Logeman, and Wheeler, 155, and for other examples of true double negatives *cf.* Zimmer, Streifzuge, 90; Eva Channing, J.A.O.S., 12, XCIX; Gebauer, Archiv f. Slav. Phil., 8, 177; Kent, Pub. Mod. Lang. Asso., 5, 190; Richardson, Harvard Studies, I, 154; Spurrel, Welsh Grammar, 158; Habich, De neg. usu Plaut., 6; Lucilius, ed. Müller, 241. But the collocation *neque . . . haud* can neither be classed with the examples of contamination, as Strong, Logeman, and Wheeler, nor with *neque . . . numquam*, as Habich would have it (see below p. 27). Habich's separation of *neque . . . numquam* from cases like *non . . . nemini* seems to me to be an arbitrary classification.

In favor of the second explanation, that proposed by Per Persson, are the numerous analogies furnished by negatives which have become such from being used to intensify negatives. The fact, too, that the use of *caná* as a positive intensive dies out in the later Vedic period, except with derivatives of *ka*, indicates that the development was from positive to negative. It may well be, however, that the resemblance in form of *caná*, "indeed," and *ca . . . na*, "and not," assisted in the development of meaning of the former. The correspondences of *caná* elsewhere speak strongly for the positive as the original force of the word; compare Av. *cina*, O.H.G. *-gin*, "irgend," O.N. *-gi*.[1] Only in the last does a negative meaning appear, and there the other Germanic dialects show the negative meaning to be a developed one.

Skr. *nū̆* as a negative was mostly used with *cid* (*nu cid*, "never"), *i. e.*, *nu* was a temporal negative adverb. The more common and doubtless earlier meaning of *nū̆* was "now," with which meaning, or with one easily connected therewith, its cognates appear in various languages: Gr. *vǔ*, Lat. *nu-(dius)*, O.Ir. *nu no*, O.H.G. *nū no*, Lith. *nu-gi*, and in Umb. *nurpener*[2] (from *nu-arpener*). In Sanskrit it is found used with a force easily derivable from that of the temporal adverb, viz., as an intensive: *ná nú nanú*, "surely not."[3] It was undoubtedly from this use as an intensive that the negative force came to be attached to the *nu*[4] in the same way in which French *pas* became negative. Other analogies will be given under the Greek negatives.

Skr. *a- an-* (negative prefix), I.E. *n̥- n̥n-*.

AVESTAN.

Av. *mā*, I.E. *mē*.

Av. *moiṭ* is formed by the addition to *mā* of the particle *iṭ*, as in the case of *noiṭ* (Skr. *nēd*, Aryan *naíd*). Probably, however,

[1] *Cf.* Brugmann, II, 241; Hübschmann, K.Z., 24, 328, n. 2; Bartholomae, Arische Forsch., II, 126; Jackson, Av. Gram., § 30; Per Persson as above; Scherer, Z.G.D.S., 475. But Goth. *-hun* is probably from I.E. stem *qu-;* J. Schmidt, K.Z., 32, 402.

[2] Brugmann, Osk. und Umbr., 225 f. In regard to Umbr. *nosve* see below (p. 29).

[3] *E. g.*, R.V., I, 165, 9, *nákir nú ná tvā́nām asti.* For the use of the temporal adverb as an intensive *cf.* Eng. *never* emphatic for *no*.

[4] But *cf.* Kretschmer, K.Z., 31, 365.

it was formed after the analogy of *noiţ* rather than by a direct union of the elements *mā* and *iţ*.

In Av. *māda* is to be seen *mā* + a pronominal stem *da* (I.E. *da*), as in *naē-da* (I.E. *nei* or *noi* + *da*).

I.E. *nĕ* probably does not occur in Av. except in compounds. The single place in which it has been supposed to occur is Yasna, 44, 19. Tradition, however, has taken the word *nā* here as the nominative of *nar*, "man," and it seems hardly probable that this negative should occur once and only once in the entire literature. The common *noiţ* appears in the preceding line. The absence of the uncompounded *nă* in O.P. also argues somewhat against the supposition of its appearance here.[1]

The common negative both in the Gathas and later Avesta is *noiţ*, corresponding to Skr. *nēd*.

I.E. *nĕ* further appears in the compound *nava* of the later Avesta and *navāţ*, "minime," "neither," of the Gathas.

Av. *naē-*, I.E. *nei* or *noi*.

Av. *naēda* (Gatha *naēda*) is I.E. *nei* or *noi* strengthened by *-da*[2] (*cf. madā*). It could hardly be the more common *noiţ* with added *-a*, as this is properly a postposition which becomes attached to cases.[3] A remnant of the (probably Avestan) use of *naē* as an independent negative adverb is seen in *naē-ciš*, "no one."

Av. *a- an-* (negative prefix), I.E. *ṇ- ṇn-*.

In a few cases also a prefix *ana-* occurs — in *ana-hvareta*, *ana-hvarepa*, *anazāpa*, *anamareždika*. If, as has been claimed above, the I.E. negative prefixes *ṇ ū̆*, indicated by the ordinary negative prefixes of the various languages, are simply the weak ablaut forms of I.E. *ne nĕ no nō*, then, it is plain, we must seek an explanation for Av. *ana-* other than as a variant form[4] of I.E. *ṇ ū̆*. The dissyllabic forms of the several languages must be considered together. In Ossetan[5] the common negative prefix is *ana-*, though *a-* also occurs; in Gr. we have a few cases of ἀνα-, ἀνάρελπτος. ἀνάρεδνος. etc.; in Prakrit Goldschmidt[6] has noted several cases of *ana-*; in

[1] *Cf.* Jolly, Ver. Syn., 33; Spiegel, Comm. 2, 358.

[2] *Cf.* Per Persson, I.F., 249.

[3] Jackson, Av. Gram., 222; Johansson, B.B., 20, 96.

[4] *Cf.* Johansson, B.B., 15. 310; J. Schmidt, K.Z., 23, 273; Kretschmer, K.Z., 31, 408.

[5] Hübschmann, Osset. Spr., 21.

[6] K.Z., 24, 426.

O.H.G. we have the single case of *una-* in *una-holda;* and Zimmer[1] has claimed that *ana-* appears in the Celtic *an-*. The O.H.G. *una-* indicates that the first element was I.E. *ṇn-*, and the simplest explanation of the presence of the *-a-*, in most cases at least, is that it has been "clipped" from the nouns having *a-* initial. The process may have taken place in proethnic times or, more probably, in the separate developments. An example of such a clipping may be seen in Mod.Ir. *am-h-*.[2] For the Celtic Zimmer supposes that *ana-* arose before sonants (*cf.* O.Ir. *bunad*, Lat. *fundus*).

OLD PERSIAN.

O.P. *mā*, I.E. *mē*.

O.P. *mātya*, "that not," is *mā* + *-tya*, the neuter accusative of a relative stem.[3]

O.P. *naiy*, I.E. *neị* or *noị*.

O.P. *naiy* may be, however, from Aryan *naịd* (Skr. *nḗd*, Av. *nōiṭ*). The presence in Iranian of I.E. *neị noị*, in Av. *naḗda* and *naḗ-ciš*, favors the connection with I.E. *neị* or *noị*.

O.P. *a-* (negative prefix), I.E. *ṇ-*.

ARMENIAN.

Arm. *mi*, I.E. *mē*.[4]

This is the only one of the I.E. negatives appearing in Arm.

The ordinary negative in Arm. is *oč*, and the modern language has also *če*. The connection[5] of Arm. *oč* and Gr. *οὐκ* has been disputed by Hübschmann. Lagarde, however, connected the two negatives, and Bugge has done the same, seeing no difficulty in the Arm. *-č* and deriving the Arm. *o-* from *ō-* from *au*, which he takes as an ablaut form[6] of the *ou* in Gr. *οὐκ*.

Inasmuch as Gr. *οὐκ* is made up of *οὐ* and an added element *-κ(ι)*, the consideration of the connection of the two negatives

[1] K.Z., 24, 523 f.

[2] *Cf.* Zimmer, K.Z., 24, 536. In Gr. ἀνάποινος, νήποινος, ἄποινα, and ποινή are to be noted.

[3] Spiegel, Keilinschriften, 182; Whitney, 499 *a*.

[4] Brugmann, I, 71; Hübschmann, Arm. Studien, 46 and 61.

[5] *Cf.* Hübschmann, Arm. Stud.; Lagarde, Arm. Stud.; Bartholomae, Indg. Studien, II, 20 f.; Bugge, K.Z., 32, 30.

[6] *Cf.* Brugmann, II, 114; Wackernagel, K.Z., 29, 141; Solmsen, *ibid.*, 92; and Prellwitz, *sub. v.* οὐ οὐκ.

really involves two questions, viz., as to the connection of Arm. *o-* and Gr. οὐ, and of Arm. -ζ́ and Gr. κ(ι).

Bartholomae has shown that Arm. ζ́ may be from *qi*, but not *ḱi*. So -ζ́ in *oζ́* might well be for -*qi, used before words beginning with a vowel, and hence to be connected with the I.E. interrogative indefinite stem *qi* and to be compared quite directly with the Skr. indefinite particle *cid*, Av. *ciṭ*, O.P. *ciy*. The question, then, as to the connection of Arm. -ζ́ and Gr. -κ(ι) will depend upon what we consider that Gr. -κι represents.

As for the connection between *o-* and Gr. οὐ-, Bugge would suppose that Arm. *o* represents I.E. *au̯-*, and that the relation of the two particles is one of ablaut. I shall try to show that Gr. οὐ belonged to the *e:o* series.

Bugge's law of Arm. *o* from I.E. *au̯* would not, of course, exclude one of *o* from I.E. *ou̯* (or *eu̯*). Hübschmann, however, has given — with some hesitation — the representation of I.E. *ou̯* and *eu̯* in Arm. as *oy*, and Bartholomae has argued for this view at some length. But the question is not so thoroughly settled that we can overlook the comparison of Arm. *oζ́*, "not," with Gr. οὐκ(ί), "not," as tending to establish a law of Arm. *o* from I.E. *ou̯*. Further to be taken into consideration is Arm. *jōnel*, beside Skr. *hávanam*, Gr. χόανος. And again, if Arm. *sork*, Skr. *çuskas*, Gr. αὐαλέος, and Arm. *ostin*, Gr. αὐσταλέος, belong to the *a:o* series, why may not Arm. *sork* and *ostin* represent the *o*-grade? [1]

GREEK.

Gr. μή (Elean μᾱ, Bœotian μει), I.E. *mē*.

With -δε μή formed a compound μηδέ, meaning either "and not" or "not even" (*cf.* οὐδέ). A number of indefinite pronouns and adverbs were formed from (1) μή and (2) μηδέ. The second element was ἀμός, εἶς,[2] τίς, ἕτερος, or an indefinite adverb.

---

[1] *Cf.* Arm. *loganol*, Gr. λο(ϝ)έω, Lat. *lavere;* B.B., 17, 123, and Thurneysen, K.Z., 28, 154. Bugge's examples are as follows (K.Z., 32, 29): (1) *sork*, Skr *çuskas*, Av. *huška*, O.P. *uška*, Lith. *saũsas*, O.B. *suchŭ*, O.E. *sēar*, Gr. αὐαλέος; (2) *ostin*, Gr. αὐσταλέος, αὐστηρός; (3) *hoc*, Gr. πιφαύσκω; (4) *oζ́*, Gr. οὐκ, *cf.* Lat. *haud* (**aud?*); (5) *p'ok'r*, Lat. *paucus*. *Cf.* further Bartholomae, B.B., XVII, 100 f.; Hübschmann, Arm. Stud., 59, 62, 78; Osthoff, Perfect, 484 ff.

[2] Breal (Mem. Soc. Ling., I, 205) thinks that μηδείς and οὐδείς contain the pronominal stem *do-*, a supposition quite possible if we consider μηδείς and οὐδείς by themselves, but considered in connection with μηδαμός, etc., μηδόλως, μηδέποτε, etc., unlikely. It would seem that, whatever the origin of οὐδείς and μηδείς, ὀδεῖνα is to be in some way connected (*cf.* Brugmann, Gr. Gr., § 94.)

I.E. *ne* does not occur in Greek as a negative adverb or as a
negative prefix. The words so explained by J. Baunack[1] are to
be accounted for otherwise. The list is ἄνευ, ἀνεμώλιος, νέκταρ,
νεβρός, and νέποδες. The last word has already been discussed ;
ἄνευ, which, as Baunack supposes, contains two negatives — a
thing thoroughly improbable —, will be discussed later on (p. 33).
As for ἀνεμώλιος it is impossible here to support the presence of
two negative prefixes in the sense of one. A comparison with
ἀνάεδνος ἀνάελπτος is useless, for here, too, we cannot suppose two
negatives, and the prefix ἀνα- is to be explained otherwise.[2] The
word seems to be connected with ἄνεμος.[3] As for νέκταρ, the word
is not I.E., but a Semitic loan word (Semitic *niqtar*).[4] With
νέβρος, which Baunack connects with βόρα, must be considered
νέβραξ, "fawn," "a young animal," νεβρῆ (with δορά), "belonging
to a fawn," νεβρίς, "a fawn skin." The absence of etymological
connection with any word for "deer" and the more general
meaning sometimes attached to νέβραξ[5] indicate that the original
meaning was a more general one than "fawn;" but that the
word was originally an adjective there is no indication. Probably
we have in νέβρος a *-ro-* suffix and the other words formed from
this by analogy — νέβραξ after πόρταξ, νέβρις after πόρτις, and the
meaning later changed from "fawn" to "fawn skin" (used as a
garment). Now if we see in νέβρος ("*descendant," "*offspring")
a root *neb-*, we shall be inclined to connect this with the root *nep-*
which I have claimed appears in νέποδες, etc. A root not difficult
to connect with these in meaning, but with a still different consonant, is *nebh-*, Skr. *nabh-*, "to rend asunder," *nabhana*, "a
spring."[6]

[1] Studien, 271 f., and *cf.* Brugmann, Gr. Gr., 223; Wheeler, Cl. Review,
III, 130, and Olavsky, "Die nhd. Partikel nicht, etc.," reviewed by Michaelis,
K.Z., VI, 309.

[2] See p. 8.

[3] *Cf.* Prellwitz, *sub v.* ἄνεμος.

[4] *Cf.* Keller, Lat. Volksetymologie, 226, and the index ; Muss-Arnolt, Trans.
Am. Ph. Assoc., 23, 143.

[5] *Cf.* Hesych. νέβρακες · οἱ ἄρρενες νεττοὶ τῶν ἀλεκτρυόνων.

[6] For variations in root determinatives between *p* — *b* *cf.* Skr. *vépate*: Lat.
vibrare, Per Persson, Wrzlw., 49, but *cf.* Fay, A.J.P., 73, 481. Variation between
p, *b*, *bh* is to be seen, *e. g.*, in *stā-b-*, *stā-bh-*, *stā-p-*, Per Persson, 59. In regard
to *nep-* and *nebh-* *cf.* Spiegel, K.Z., 13, 370, and 19, 392. See also Brugmann,
I, 469, 7. Lat. *nefrens*, if it means "young," may also belong here, in which
case we should have the roots *nep-*, *neb-*, *nebh-* in three words meaning "offspring."

The common negative in Greek taking the place of the lost I.E. *ne* is οὐ, the origin and connection of which has never been very satisfactorily explained.[1] It was suggested by Bopp [2] that Gr. οὐ is connected with the pronominal stem seen in Av. *ava*. He conceived that not only Gr. οὐ, but Skr. *na* and other negatives as well, had developed their negative meaning from a demonstrative one of *remoteness*.

The most serious attempt to find a derivation for οὐ has been made by Henry,[3] who attempts to connect οὐ directly with the Skr. preposition *ava-*. To make this connection Henry sets up *oua-* as the I.E. form of the preposition, and by so doing is compelled both to reject Brugmann's law of the Skr. treatment of I.E. *o* in open syllables,[4] and, on account of Lat. *au-*, to accept Thurneysen's [5] law of *ou* to *au* in Lat. That a prefix with a "sens inversif" may become practically a negative prefix may be admitted, and perhaps the best example [6] is Lith. *be-*, O.B. *bez(ŭ)-*, used as a negative prefix, compared with Skr. *bahis*, "out," "outward." But there is no example by any means sure of a case where such a prefix has become a true negative adverb.[7] Henry himself intimates that the strongest argument in favor of his derivation is that no other seems to be at hand.

It seems certain that the negative meaning of Gr. οὐ is an acquired one. This being so, it would be good method, if we are to seek a derivation for οὐ, to note the ways in which such an acquisition of negative force has been made in the case of other words not originally negative. We may classify as follows :

1. Negatives formed by composition of I.E. *mē* or *ne* with some other word do not concern us, except as they show that with negatives intensives were often used which sometimes coa-

---

[1] Grimm, Deutsche Gram., III, 759, and Pott, Ety. Forsch., I, 405–8, have discussed the origin of the Gr. negative, but hardly in a way satisfactory to the modern philologist. Hartung's explanation (see Bopp) I have not seen.

[2] Ver. Gram., III, §§ 371, 379, and Scherer, Z.G.D.S., 331.

[3] Mem. Soc. Ling., 6, 378, and *cf.* Brugmann, Gr. Gr., § 164, and the Nachträge; Planer, De Neg. Haud, and others.

[4] See now Streitberg, I.F., III, 364.

[5] K.Z., 28, 154 f.

[6] *Cf.* Lat. *exlex*, "lawless" (Lucilius, frag. 22, Müller), Skr. *vi-hasta*, "without hands," etc., Skr. *nir-bhara*, "without measure," etc.

[7] On Alb. *-s* see p. 18.

lesced with the negative. Examples are Skr. *nanū*, O.H.G. *niwiht*, and in I.E itself *nei̯*.

2. Words of certain semasiological categories may *develop* a negative meaning from the original: (*a*) Words meaning "away from," "other," or the like, *e. g.*, M.H.G. *anders*, *ander*, *mēre* (in sense of "weiter"), *baz* and *furbaz*;[1] (*b*) comparatives or superlatives, or even positives, having a diminutive force, *e. g.*, Lat. *minus* and *minime* (*minus* especially in *quo minus*), O.E. *med-* in *med-wis*, etc. It is to be noted here, however, that, possibly with the exception of Alb. *s* (Lat. *dis- ?*), none of the examples shows the development of a full-fledged negative adverb.

3. Words which from their meaning may be closely connected with a negative may take on a negative force not by development from their own proper meaning, but from *association*. These words are more or less plainly indefinite pronouns or adverbs, and at the same time more or less plainly intensives of the negative with which they are used.[2] The following is a list of negative pronouns and adverbs which have become negative by association. Doubtless others could be added.[3]

In M.H.G.[4] *dekein*, *kein*, and *deweder* could be used either with or without *niht* to give a negative force to the sentence; hence the negative force of *kein* and *weder* in N.H.G. In O.N. *en-ge*, "Niemand" (*cf.* Goth. *ni ains-hun*), *man(n)-ge*, "Niemand," *hver-ge*, "nirgends" (*cf.* O.S. *ni hver-gin*), and *vaettr*, "nichts," but also "etwas" (*cf.* Goth. *ni waihts*). In O.Bohemian[5] *zadny* from meaning "desideratus" came to mean "nullus," and *kto* from meaning "aliquis" came to mean "nemo." In O.Ir. *nach na*, "ullus" "aliquis," is also found with meaning "nullus." In Welsh[6] *nef*, *dim*, and *byth* are either positive or negative indefi-

---

[1] Paul, M.H.G. Gram., 125. In Albanian *-s* (*-z*) became a quite commonly used negative, and, if it were really from Lat. *dis-*, would be the best example of this sort of development. Particles giving a bad signification may deserve mention here. *Cf.* Skr. *dus-*, Gr. δυς-, Arm. *t-* ; O.Ir. *mi-*, Germ. *miss-*.

[2] No line can be drawn between the two classes. It is to be noted, too, that some nouns, *e. g.*, *res* and *homo*, may be used practically as indefinite pronouns.

[3] *Cf.* Paul, M.H.D. Gram., 124.

[4] *Cf.* Grimm, Deutsche Gram., III, 720; Paul, M.H.D. Gram., 125; and Hahn, M.H.D. Gram., § 435 f.

[5] Gebauer, Archiv f. Slav. Phil., 7, 188.

[6] Spurrel, Welsh Gram., 159.

nites. French *rien*, "nothing," (Lat. *rem*) got its negative meaning from association.

Skr. *nu*, "not," *nu cid*, "never," I have mentioned above as
taking its regular force from association with *na*. I have also
followed Per Persson in supposing a similar origin of the negative
force in Skr. *cana*. Lat. *haud*, which I believe belongs here, will
be discussed below. French *pas*[1] and *point* are well known as
examples of this phenomenon. Italian *mica miga*, Provençal
mica miga mia, O.French *mie*[2] (Lat. *mīca*) show the same shift in
meaning as *pas* and *point*. Modern Gr. διόλου has its negative
meaning from use as intensive to a negative.

It is to be noted, then, that the use of intensives with negatives is common; that sometimes this intensive united with the
negative to form a compound; but that it quite frequently became
a negative itself; and that of negative adverbs not connected with
mē or *ne*, and whose etymology we know, *all*, with the possible
exception of Alb. *-s*, *came into use as intensives to negatives*.[3] We
should do well, then, to suppose that the same thing took place
in the case of Gr. οὐ which we know took place in the case of
French *pas*.[4]

In searching for a connection for Gr. οὐ among words that
could be used as intensives we will hardly find the object of our
search among the names of diminutive objects (*passus, whit*, etc.),
but rather among more generally used intensives, more or less
closely connected with pronominal stems like Skr. *nu* and I.E.
ĭ. Such a particle seems to be at hand in the Skr. *ū̆*.[5]

[1] In the Creole of the Antilles French *ne* has entirely disappeared, and *pa* by
itself is the ordinary word for "not." *Cf.* de Poyen-Bellisle, "Les Sons et les
Formes du Créole dans les Antilles, 50.

[2] O'Connor, A.J.P., 2, 210.

[3] The development of the conjunctionally used negatives, Goth. *ibai* and
O.B. *jeda*, is in reality the syntactical development of the clauses introduced by
those particles. Probably in both of these cases the development was from an
indirect question to a clause of fear to a final clause.

[4] On the general connection between intensives and negatives *cf.* Strong,
Logeman, and Wheeler, Hist. of Lang., 102. Other words may obtain a new
force in the same way — *cf.* the Italian *cosa* with interrogative force from use
with *che*.

[5] On this particle *cf.* Fick, B.B., 7, 270; Osthoff, Perf., 328, M.U., 4, 253;
Delbrück, Syn. Forsch., 5, 504 f.; Brugmann, Gr. Gr., 224; Kretschmer, K.Z.,
31, 364; etc.

Whatever may have been the original meaning and function of
the I.E. *n̄*, the value indicated for it by the separate languages is
simply that of a *particle* with no more definite value than that of
a mere intensive or at most of a demonstrative.   In general it is
very similar to *ī*.   In giving the occurrences I assume that the
word belongs in the *e:o* ablaut series.[1]   For the positive side of
the argument in favor of this the examples given will themselves
be all the evidence obtainable.   It may be noted here, however,
that the supposition that a given weak form belongs in the *e:o*
series is antecedently more probable than that it belongs to any
other.[2]

The particle in proethnic times could become attached to
words.   The locative plural endings *-si* and *-su* were evidently
formed from *-s* by the additions of the particles *-i* and *-u*.[3]   Bartholomae[4] supposes also that there was a locative singular suffix *-u*
beside that in *-i*.   The examples, though few and only adverbs,
show an I.E. use of the particle whether the words affected were
full-fledged case forms or not.

The union of *-u* with the pronoun *so-* is doubtless I.E.[5]   This
use of *-u* is paralleled by the more frequent employment of *-i* in
the formation of pronouns: Lat. *qui*, etc.[6]

The particle was attached to the third person singular and
plural secondary endings (*-t-u*, *-nt-u*).[7]   Here, too, there is a
parallelism with the particle *-i*, if it is the latter that differentiates
the " primary" from the "secondary" endings.[8]

[1] On ablaut of particles *cf.* Osthoff, Perfect., 328, and Per Persson, I.F., 200 f.

[2] Osthoff (Perf. 328), however, sees the strong form of Skr. *n̄* in Gr. αὖ, and
so others — a view which Brugmann (Gr. Gr., 221) questions and Kretschmer
(K.Z., 31, 364) argues against.   Sonne (K.Z., 12, 278) suggests the comparison
of Gr. αὖ and Skr. *ū* (*a + u*): *cf.* Prellwitz, *sub v.* αὖ and αὐερύω.

[3] Brugmann, II, 356.

[4] B.B., 15, 23, and *cf.* Brugmann, II, 256, Rem.

[5] Skr. *so a-sāu* (for both genders), Av. *hāu* (for both genders), O.P. *hauv*
(for both genders), Gr. οἷ-τος.   *Cf.* Brugmann, Gr. Gr., 130; Delbrück, Syn.
Forsch., IV, 139; Sonne, K.Z., 12, 270, and Windisch, Curtius Studien, 2, 263
and 366 f.   It is possible that Gr. οὗτος is for **so-utos, cf.* Skr. *uta*, but the other
view seems preferable.   The use of *u* after pronouns and even between pronouns is common in Skr.

[6] *Cf.* Per Persson, I.F., II, 247 f.

[7] Brugmann, II, 992, 1017; Thurneysen, K.Z., 27, 174; Hirt, I.F., I, 206;
Osthoff, M.U., IV, 252, 257.

[8] Brugmann, II, 909, 973.

An I.E. compound arising from the collocation of two particles is to be seen in Skr. *ŏ* (beside the simple *ā*), Gr. *aŭ*, Lat. *au-t(i) au-tem*, Osc. av-ti *av-ti*, Umbr. u-te *o-te*, Goth. *au-k*, O.N. *au-k*, O.E. *eá-c*, O.S. *ō-k*, O.H.G. *ou-h*. I shall attempt to show (p. 33) that the Gr., Goth., and O.H.G. words for "without," *ἄνευ, inu, āno*, contain the particle *u-*, in the case of the Gr. in the strong form *eu*. The compound would be of much the same sort as the one just mentioned. If I am right in claiming that *ἄνευ* contains the strong form of I.E. *u*, it is plain the particle belongs in the *e:o* ablaut series, and forms of the *o-* grade may be expected.

I.E. *u* appears in the Skr. intensive and conjunctional particle *u*,[1] and in composition in *san-u-tar*[2] (beside *san-i-tur*), and *u-ta* — an Aryan formation (Av. *uta*, O.P. *uta*). In Gr. the weak form of the particle appears in *πάν-υ*[3] and the *o-* strong grade form probably in *οὖν*. In Latin our particle is probably to be seen in *ne-u, se-u, ce-u*.[4] In Goth. *-u* appears as an interrogative particle[5] and in connection with *-h* (*-uh*) as a conjunctional and intensive particle. O.B. *u-* in *u-bo* "*οὖν*" is perhaps to be compared with Gr. *οὖ* of *οὖ-v*.

I hold it to be reasonably certain, (1) that Gr. *οὐ* received its negative force from use as an intensive, (2) that the particle whose weak form is *u* was capable of being used as an intensive, and (3) that it could have the ablaut form *ou*. Positive evidence in Gr. itself that *οὐ* did so get its negative force would consist of a use corresponding to the common one of (*ne*) . . . *pas* in French; but one negative- possibly the only one -- from which *οὐ* derived its negative meaning died out before historical times, and *οὐ* having become a full-fledged negative, we ought not to expect to

---

[1] Delbrück, Syn. Forsch., 5, 504 f.

[2] Gr. *ἄτερ*, Goth. *sundrō*, etc., show the word without the particle. Arm. *ev* probably does not belong here; cf. Hübschmann, Arm. Stud., 75; Brugmann, I, 63.

[3] Osthoff, M.U., IV, 252; Brugmann, Gr. Gr., 130.

[4] Of these *neu* may be a form of *nĕve*, but *seu* is not from *si-ve*, and *ceu* is unexplained. *Ce-u* contains the pronominal deictive stem *k̑o-k̑e-* seen in *ce-ce* and elsewhere, and *sĕ-* in *seu* is the pronominal stem seen in the preposition *sē* (*sēd*), "without," in the conjunction *sed*, and in the reflexive pronoun *se; cf.* Stolz, Lat. Gr., 346; Per Persson, I.F., II, 223; v. Planta, 145.

[5] Cf., however, Liden quoted by Per Persson, I.F., II, 213. J. Schmidt (Vocalismus, I, 152), Sonne (K.Z., XII, 289), and Scherer (Z.G.D.S., 374) identify Goth. *-u* and Skr. *u*.

find it used as an intensive, except perchance in some construction or collocation of words which would in some way protect οἴ
from being taken as a negative.[1]

Strengthened forms[2] of Gr. οὐ are οὐκί and οὐχί and their ante-
vocalic forms οὐκ and οὐχ. Of οὐκί and οὐχί it is possible that
only οὐκί is original, and that οὐχί arose by a sort of proportional
analogy between οὐκ, οὐχ' (before vowel with rough breathing),
and οὐκί. More probably, however, we have in the -χι of οὐχί the
correspondent of Skr. *hi*,[3] Av. *zī*,[4] "for," "certe," O.B. *zi*, I.E.
$\hat{g}hi$. In Skr., Av., and O.B. the word is used as an intensive; so
also in Gr. besides οὐχί in ἦχι and ναίχι.

The -κι of οὐ-κί is generally considered as the same particle
that appears in ναί-κι and πολλά-κι and other multiplicatives.
Wackernagel and J. Schmidt have connected this with Skr. *cid*,
I.E. pronominal stem *qi*-, to which Brugmann and Osthoff
objected that the particle would appear as -τι, and they therefore
connected it with a stem $\hat{k}i$. It can hardly be claimed that the
u element of the velar was lost in enclisis, as Bechtel has suggested, and so that dentalization did not take place, for we should
have to dispose of τέ, Lat. *que*, Skr. *ca*, and besides it is improbable, though not impossible, that an enclitic word should have a
different treatment from an unaccented syllable (*cf.* πέντε).[5]

Gr. ναίκι[6] is either a barbarism for ναίχι or a transformation of

[1] It is possible that we are to see survivals of the original force of οὐ in the
collocation οὐκ οἴ ν (positive) and in the οὐ μή constructions, otherwise explained
by Goodwin (Moods and Tenses, Appendix II).

[2] Their occurrences in Homer are: οὐ, 1336; οὐκ, 464; οὐχ, 27; οὐκί, 15,
and οὐχί, 2 (O 716 = II 762). Among other occurrences of οὐχί Herodas has
twelve cases; *cf.* Smyth, Ionic Dialect, 295.

[3] Osthoff, M.U., IV, 239 f.; Pott, Wurzelwörterbuch, I, 1567.

[4] Av. *yezi* has been explained by Bartholomae (Ar. Forsch., II, 8, n. 3, and
cf. Osthoff, M.U., 4, 240) as from *yad* + *zī* (*i. e.*, *yadghī*), and he compares
uzūipiōi. But the cases are not necessarily similar, since *uzūipiōi* may have
been formed after *ud*- became *uz*- in Av. A better explanation, it seems to me,
is that **yedi*, "when," "if," was changed to *yezi* under the influence of *zi*, "if,"
but without the original form being driven entirely out of existence, so that we
still have in the younger Av. *yeďi*, "if," the direct descendant of an earlier **yedi*.

[5] *Cf.* Wackernagel, K.Z., 25, 286 f.; Osthoff, M.U., IV, 241 f.; J. Schmidt,
Pluralbildung, 252; Bechtel, Hauptprobleme, 354; Brugmann, II, 409, Gr. Gr.,
131; Solmsen, K.Z., 33, 298 f.; de Saussure, Mem. Soc. Ling., 6, 161; and
Buck, I.F., 4, 156.

[6] Aristophanes, Thesm., 1183, 1218.

ναίχι under the influence of οὐκί. The -κ- in οὐκί, in the -κι of πολλάκι and other multiplicatives, and that in the troublesome indefinite and interrogative forms of various dialects, probably have a common explanation.   In the case of οὐκί considered by itself there is no reason for not supposing that the -κ- is from an original velar after the *u*.[1]   The connection of -κ- in οὐκί with a velar is preferable for several reasons: 1) It permits of a direct connection of -κι with Skr. *cid*, Av. *ci*, O.P. *ciy*, which have a similar use.   2) The I.E. pronominal stem *ki* is rare, and we have no evidence of its use as a particle.   3) Gr. -κι in οὐκί will then be connected directly with Arm. č̣ of oč̣, and, if Arm. *o* may be from I.E. *ou*, Gr. οὐκί, "not," will be connected directly with Arm. oč̣, "not."

Considering the very great frequency with which negatives are used with indefinites, there seems to be no possible objection to supposing with Solmsen that the -κ- of the troublesome indefinite forms arose in the same way — in connection with οὐ.   And a similar explanation is at hand for the -κι of πολλάκι and other multiplicatives, if we suppose that -κι arose in *πολυ-κι (I.E. *pllū qi(d)*, Skr. *purū cid*) and was thence transferred to a stem πολλα- of other adverbs.   Having become established as a multiplicative suffix, it was added also to stems of numerals, possibly displacing an earlier -τι(s) (*cf.* Taren. ἁμάτις, "once").[2]

The compounds formed of οὐ and δέ are analogous to those formed of μή and δέ.

Gr. αν-[3] α- (negative prefixes), I.E. *n̥- n̥n-*.

Gr. νη-, Doric νᾱ (negative prefix), I.E. *n̥̄*.

ALBANIAN.

Alb. *mo-* (in *mo-s*), I.E. *mē*.

Alb. *nenge, nenk, nuk* Meyer derives from the Lat. *numquam*.

Alb. *s* (before voiced consonants *z*) Meyer derives from Lat.

---

[1] Brugmann, I, 427 ; de Saussure, Mem. Soc. Ling., 6, 161.

[2] Brugmann now accepts the view that the -κ- of πολλά-κι and of the indefinites is from the velar, the peculiar treatment being due to enclisis.   He explains the dentalization in the enclitic τέ as due to the retention of the *u* element of the particle (*kue*) when used before words beginning with an accented vowel — *e* being elided and *ku*- really forming part of an accented syllable. Berichten der Königl. Sächs. Gesellschaft der Wissenschaften, 1895, 32 f.

[3] In regard to ἀνα- *cf.* p. 8.

dis-.   But this *-s* is the same that appears in *mo-s*,[1] which would seem to preclude the possibility of a connection with a word of negative or quasi-negative meaning.   It at the same time indicates that the origin of the negative *s* was in an intensive to a negative.   Compare with Alb. *mo-s:s* Skr. *nanú:nu* ("not").

LATIN.

Lat. *nē*, I.E. *nē*.

Lat. *nē* formed various compounds: 1) Loose compounds with conjunctions, *nēdum*, *nēve*, *neu* (**nēu*) (?); 2) more or less close compounds with various indefinites, *nēcubi*,[2] *nēcunde*, *nēquis*, with conjunctional force of *nē; nēquam*, *nēquiter*, *nēquitia*, *nēquā-quam*, and *nē . . . quidem*, in which *nē* appears with no conjunctional or prohibitive value.

Lat. *ne*, I.E. *ne*.

The simple *ne* written as a separate word is, of course, not common.[3]   But the *ne-* in *nescio*[4] and *nequeo* is to be regarded as the retention of an independent negative with these particular verbs, and the conjunctional negatives *neque* and *nisi*[4] show the particle restricted in application, but hardly in meaning.   I prefer to follow O. Brugmann[5] in deriving *nisi* from *nesei*, which form appears on the inscription from Spoleto.   It is hardly possible that the original form was **neisi*[6] and that the *ei i* has been shortened before *-si* as an enclitic.   Such a shortening, especially in dissyllabic words, seems hardly well established.   *Sine*[7] and *quoque*[8] cannot be adduced as examples.   It would seem that the law of shortening, if it existed, would apply to *nēve* and *nēdum* as readily as to **neisi*.   Moreover, in Sen. Cons. de Bacch., which is older than the change of *ei* to *ī*, we have *nisei*.   The change of

[1] So Meyer, Alb. Wört., *sub v. mos*.

[2] Lucan, 9, 1059, shows the *e* of *nēcubi* to be long.

[3] For the occurrences of *ne cf.* Lorenz' note to Plautus, Most., 110; Dräeger, Hist. Syn., I, 133; and Habich, De neg. usu Plaut.

[4] *Nesapius* (Petronius, 50, 5) is formed in imitation of *nescius* (from *nescio*). *cf.* also Terentius Scaurus, De orthogr. Gr. Lat., VII, 12, 4.

[5] O. Brugmann, Ni., 33, and *cf.* Lindsay, Lat. Gr., 611.

[6] *Cf.* Wackernagel, Gr. Ak., 22; Skutsch, Forsch. Lat. Gr., 9, and the Nachträge.

[7] Per Persson, I.F., 2, 223, n.

[8] Lindsay, Lat. Gr., 598.

e to *i* in *nisi* and *nihil* may be due to assimilation, as O. Brugmann supposes, or to a lack of accent, as Lindsay supposes for
nisi and Per Persson[1] for *sine* (from **se-ne*), *mihi*, and *tibi*, or
possibly both influences may have operated to produce the
change.

Ne further appears compounded with another particle in *nec*,
"not." The form *nec* may be a sentence doublet of *neque*, and in
its use as conjunction such is doubtless the case ; but *nec*, "non,"
has generally[2] been explained as containing a particle -*ce*. Greenough,[3] however, has attempted to explain this use of *nec* without
separating it from *neque*. Whatever may be said of the possibility of such a genesis as Greenough supposes — and I confess it
seems to me extremely improbable —, account must be taken of
the fact that *neglego, negotium, neg ritu* have *neg*, not *nec*. There
is no way of explaining a change of *c* to *g*. For these forms it
is necessary to set up a negative *neg*, and for this further support
is found in Latin in the denominative *nego* and in *negumate(?)*.
With this *neg* is to be compared directly Lith. *negi*. Further,
Havet[4] has pointed out that the form *nec* of XII Tab. may as
well be *neg* as *nec*, and the same is true of the passages in Cicero
which are imitations of old laws. It may not be difficult to
understand, too, how the formulas *nec opinans, nec recte, nec pro-
cul, res nec mancipi,* etc., remained in use after the simple *neg* had
nearly or completely died out. The -*g* may have been changed
to -*c* through influence of old orthography (legal and religious),
or through influence of the spoken *nec* conjunction (compare *neg
ritu* and *nec rite*). The few cases[5] which cannot be considered as
stereotyped formulas may show either the retention of the simple
nec (*neg*) or the extension of use from the stereotyped formulas.
The very few cases of *neque*, "non," may be the result of a still
further confusion [*nec* ("and not") : *nec* ("not") :: *neque* ("and
not") : *neque* ("not")], or more probably are copyist errors.[6]

Quin in all its uses has commonly been derived from *qui* and

[1] I.F., 2, 223.

[2] *Cf.* Habich, De neg. Plaut., 31 and references.

[3] Harvard Studies, 2, 129 f.

[4] Mem. Soc. Ling., 6, 118.

[5] For examples see Greenough and Habich as above.

[6] *Cf.* Havet, Mem. Soc. Ling., 6, 118, n. Probably -*que* for -*c* is to be seen
in the form **doneque* (*donique*) for *donec*.

the negative *ne*, but Wharton has derived the conjunction from *qui* + *num*, and Per Persson[1] has claimed that the *quin* of *alioquin, ceteroquin, atquin*, and *hercle quin* contains the positive particle *ne*.

Sin does not contain a negative.[2]

Ne also forms negative indefinite adverbs and pronouns: *neutiquam, neutique* (late), *neuter, nunquam, nusquam, nūllus*. With the exception of *nūllus* the simplex of these compounds begins with *u-* from I.E. *qu-*,[3] and the initial velar should appear in compounds as in *ali-cubi* and *nē-cubi*. *Neutiquam* and *neuter* may be regarded as transformates of older compounds with the *-c-* or as being formed after I.E. *qu-* had become *u-*. The existence of the form *necuter*[4] renders the first supposition probable for *neuter*. Moreover *neuter* in contrast to *neutiquam* was pronounced in early Latin with *neu-* forming two syllables.[5] It was, then, a compound transformed from the compound *ne-cuter* under the influence of the simplex *uter*. The absence of contraction in this case was due probably to the accent on the *ne*. Possibly also the side form *necuter* exerted an influence.

In early Latin *neutiquam* was regularly pronounced with the first syllable short.[6] This can mean nothing else, it seems to me, than that *neutiquam* was a collocation of two words[7] and so pronounced with elision of the final *-e* or, more properly speaking, with slurring[8] of final *-e* and initial *u-*. This collocation, formed simply by the juxtaposition of negative *ne* and the indefinite *utiquam*, remained after the use of the simplex *utiquam* had died out.   Later the collocation suffered contraction and became a compound.

[1] I.F., 2, 212.

[2] Per Persson, I.F., 2, 222.

[3] *Cf.* J. Schmidt, K.Z., 32, 394 f.

[4] C.I.L., VI, 1527; Lucretius, 4, 1217 (where read *nec*, not *neque*), 5, 839; Mart., 5, 20, 11.   *Cf.* J. Schmidt, K.Z., 32, 403.

[5] Lindsay, Lat. Lang., 143.

[6] Lindsay, Lat. Lang., 143; Lorenz to Mil., 631, and Brix to Capt., 586.

[7] Otherwise, Brugmann, I.F., 6, 84.

[8] That the Romans so pronounced is indicated by analogies of modern speech. *Cf.* also Probus (apud Gellius, XIII, 21, 6), who says that *turrim* had a more melodious sound than *turrem* in *turrim in præcipiti stantem*.   See Lindsay, Lat. Lang., 144.

In the case of *nunquam* and *nusquam*, while earlier forms with -*cu*- may have existed, the compounds as they appear have no direct connection with those possible earlier forms. *Nunquam* and *nusquam* and *nūllus* are generally considered as showing composition with elision of -*e* of the negative. The other examples given by Stolz[1] as showing elision may be explained otherwise. *Noenum* will be treated below, *nūtiquam*, so far as I know, does not occur, *sorsus* is from *se-vorsūs,[2] and *sūdūs* may have been formed in Italic times and so the *ū* be from -*ou*- and that from -*eu*-. An explanation of *nunquam*, *nusquam*, and *nūllus* which should not need to suppose an elision would seem desirable. In the case of *nūllus*, since *ūllus* never had an initial consonant, there is no difficulty in supposing it to be from *noullus from *ne-ullus. Later, when the initial of *unquam* and *usquam* came to agree with that of *ūllus* — save possibly in quantity — *nunquam* and *nusquam* would be natural analogical formations[3] (*ūllus : nūllus :: unquam : nunquam*).

It is to be noted that neither *ne* nor *nē* in any of the compounds mentioned is a true negative prefix. Each is used to form negative indefinite adverbs or pronouns. Similarly *ne* enters into the compounds *nēmo* and *nihilum* from *ne-hemo[4] and *ne-hīlum.[5] But we have two or three[6] words which appear to have *ne*- as a prefix. If *nefrens* meant "a young animal just weaned," it may have been some sort of a corruption of Gr. νεβρός, "a fawn," or

---

[1] Lat. Gr., 276, Anm. Brugmann (I.F., 6, 80) also derives *numquam* from *n'unquam*. If *mult'angulus*, given by Brugmann, I, 604, and *multanimis* were true examples of elision, they would not really affect the argument here, for these words are compounds of another sort — the first member is a stem, while compounds of *ne* are the result of *sentence combination*. In *indipiscor*, *indago*, and the like, the first member had lost its vowel before the compound was formed. In *magnōpere* and *tantōpere* we can hardly suppose an elision of a long vowel.

[2] Solmsen, Stud. zur lat. Lautg., and *cf.* below, p. 24.

[3] There can be no difficulty with the length of the vowels. That the -*u*- of *nūllus* is long is shown by C.I.L., X, 4787. The quantity of -*u*- in *nunquam* and *nusquam* follows either that of *nūllus* or of *unquam* and *usquam*.

[4] *Cf.* Havet, Mem. Soc. Ling., 5, 447, who thinks that *nēmo* is from *nehemo from *nehomo, but that a simplex *hemo* (see Festus, 110, Müller) is a fiction of Verrius Flaccus.

[5] By assimilation of vowels as in *nisi*. The *ī*, beside *hīlum*, is from the *ī* of *nihil*, which was shortened after the dropping of -*um*.

[6] Lat. *nefrens* (?), "kidney," goes with Gr. νέφρος, etc. Brugmann, I, 423.

possibly has a root, I.E. *nebh-;*[1] but, at any rate, it can hardly mean a "not eating animal," for it was applied to animals at a time when they began to eat.[2]

It is only[3] in *nefas* and its connected adjectives[4] that we have *ne-* used practically as a true negative prefix. But doubtless this was originally an elliptical expression for *ne fas est*, used at first with more or less exclamatory force and later almost as a true noun. Its original character may be indicated by its frequent use as a parenthetical exclamation.[5] For a similar development compare *nimirum*. Somewhat similar are Skr. *nāstika* and *itihasa*.

Lat. *nō-* (in *nō-n(e)*), I.E. *nō*.

Lat. *nōn* has commonly been derived from *noenum* from *ne +* *oinom*. The derivation is impossible[6] on phonetic grounds, if we suppose that the *-o-* of the dipthong is short. But Solmsen,[7] following Thurneysen, Kretschmer, and J. Schmidt, supposes that the result of the contraction of *ne* and *oinom* was *nōinom*, and that this *long* dipthong later became *ō*. Neither of these changes is well supported.

For the law of *e–o* to *ō* the single other example brought forward is *nōlo* from *nevolo*, and the validity of this example depends upon the law which Solmsen tries to establish of the dropping out of intervocalic *v* before *o* in prehistoric Latin. For this last law the examples given are as follows:

1) *nōlō,* etc.

2) *deorsum, seorsum.*

3) *sōl < *sāol < *sāvol < *sāul.*

4) *deus < *deivos, Gnaeus < Gnaivos.*

5) *prōris < prāvoris =* Gr. πρῳρα *< πρωϝαιρα,* I.E. *pr̥vr̥iā(ī).*

I may be permitted to give reasons for thinking that, leaving

[1] *Cf.* p. 11n.

[2] References in Forcellini.

[3] Havet, Mem. Soc. Ling., 6, 108, sees *ne-* in *necesse*. The word is probably to be connected with Gr. ἔνεκ-.

[4] On confusion of derivatives of *fas* and *fāri* see Breal, Mem. Soc. Ling., 5, 339. The words seem not to have been used freely before Cicero, yet see Cato, 39, 12; 40, 7; 42, 7 (Jordan).]*astud*, C.I.L., I, 812, Conway, I.F., 4, 213, takes as *castud* and thinks the inscription not Latin.

[5] Catullus, 68, 91; Vergil, 7, 73; 8, 688.

[6] But *cf.* Osthoff, Arch. Lat. Lex., 4, 459.

[7] Solmsen, Stud. zur Lat. Lautge., 53 f.; Kretschmer, K.Z., 314, 62; J. Schmidt, K.Z., 32, 407.

nōlo out of account, the examples given lack much of proving the existence of the law, and, that so, another explanation for *nōlo* is desirable.

Prōris, if it really occurred, is best explained, as Solmsen himself thinks probable, as for *prōra* — itself borrowed from the Gr. —after the analogy of *puppis*.

Notwithstanding the Gr. transcription of *Gnaivos* without a sign for *v*, beside Ὀκταουιαν and Ἀουεντίνῳ in the Monumentum Ancyranum, the *v* in the word cannot have had a different treatment from that of *aevus, avus, fugitivus, octavus,* etc., which Solmsen necessarily supposes retained their -*v*- until after *v-o* before *s* had become *v-u*.[1] And the same remark would apply to the derivation of *deus* from **deivos*.[2]

Sōl has been derived from **sāvel* by Schulze,[3] which derivation would fall in directly with Solmsen's law[4] of *ave* to *ao* to *ō*, were it not for *novem, pover*, which show that *ve* in final syllables following the accent was not changed. But this would not prevent *sāvelis, sāvel-em,* etc., from becoming *sōlis, sōlem,* etc., after which the nom. *sōl* would be a natural analogical formation.

The forms *deorsum, seorsum, dorsum, sorsum* are best taken as formed after the analogy of *introrsus, retrorsus,*[5] etc., and the variation as due to the influence of the prepositions. Solmsen himself explains the late *extrōrsum* and *ultrorsum* by analogy. So also *horsum* is an analogical formation.

The presence in Plautus of *nevolō* and the difficulty[6] with the *eo* verbs speak somewhat against the derivation of *nōlo* and *nōlim* from *ne-volo, nevelim*. But if we once admit the presence in Lat. of a negative *nō-*, the easier derivation of *nōlo* and *nōlim* is from

[1] P. 45 f.

[2] *Cf.* Bronisch, Osk. *i*- und *e*-Vocale, 180, n.; Thurneysen, K.Z., 32, 558.

[3] K.Z., 27, 428.

[4] P. 82 ff. On the contraction of -*āo*- *cf.* Bartholomae, Stud. zur idg. Sprachgeschichte, II, 142, and Buck, Osc.-Umbr. Verb-system, 151.

[5] These from *intro-ve*- by change of -*ve*- to *o* (Solmsen, 82 f.), or from *intro-vo-, v* being dropped between like vowels (*cf.* Solmsen, 109 f.). I see no reason why, if *ovō* became *ō, ēve* became *ē, ivi* became *i,* and *ava ā,* we should not suppose that *ovo* became *ō.* Both forms, *dorsum* and *deorsum,* are found in Dec. Min., C.I.L., 1, 199. The contemporaneous use of the two forms indicates that one was not the phonetic development of the other. While Plautus has *deorsum,* it is always dissyllabic. (*Cf.* Wagner to Aul., 365.)

[6] Solmsen explains this chronologically.

no-volo, *no-velim*, or *no-volim*, against which derivation no phonetic objections can be raised.

The support for a law of *eo* to *ō*, then, seems very slight ; but starting from a form *nōinom* we still should have to show that *-ōi-* would become *ō* elsewhere than where final. Kretschmer's[1] only example in support of the law besides *pōtus pōculum* (*cf.* Skr. *pāyāna-m*), which counts for nothing when compared with Skr. *pātave pātra-m*, is this same supposed *nōinom* to *nōn(um)*. And the only other support for the law is the corresponding supposed change of *ōu* to *ō*,[2] which Solmsen himself has pretty well disposed of. Schmidt[3] has added only *prōd-*, which he supposes from *prō-id*. This is possibly an ablative case form, or has its *-d* from words beginning with that letter, to which it was prefixed. The probable explanation, however, is that *prōd-* is after the analogy of *ind-* and other prepositions ending in *-d* (*postid, antid, red*), a transformation favored by the proportion *in-* : *ind-* :: *prō-* : *prōd-*. Solmsen suggests *prōmō* as a further example. But this is to be explained as a transformation of *proemo* (or *prūmo*) under the influence of *prō*. The meanings of the simple verb and the compound had ceased to indicate the connection of the two words, while in the compound the idea of *prō* was very apparent. In much the same way *coemo* (*cūmo*) became *cōmo*, with the meaning "to bring together," while, when the compound had the meaning of the simplex, the form *coëmo* was retained without even contraction taking place. In the case of *prōmo dēmo* may have assisted in the transformation. The same sort of transformation as in *prōmō* and *cōmō* is to be seen in *sūmō* and probably in *dēgō*,[4] beside *deamāre*, etc.

The fact is that this derivation of *nōn* from *nōinum*, supported by that of *nōlō* from *nevolo*, has been the mainstay of all three suppositions just discussed. But even if it were perfectly sure

[1] K.Z., 31, 462.

[2] And *cf.* Buck, Osk. Voc., 163 ; Brugmann, Die Ausdrücke für den Begriff der Totalität, 54 ff.

[3] K.Z., 32, 407.

[4] Otherwise Stolz, Hist. Gr., 219, who considers *cōmo* as well as *dēgo* due to a regular contraction. But for *cōmō* at least we cannot suppose that the result of the contraction of *o e* was affected by the fact that the first vowel belonged to the preposition *co-*. The length of the vowel in *cōmō* may be due to *prōmō* and *dēmō*, or to the form — *coemo* — of which it was a transformate, or to both causes.

that *e-oi* could become *ōi* and *ōi ō*, we should still have to explain how, if *noenum* became *nōn*, it also remained. We have two cases of *noenum* in Lucretius (III, 198, and IV, 712), though Plautus, a century and a half before, used *nōn* far more often than *noenum*.[1] And while we find *noenum* in the early literature—not, however, in inscriptions— beside the far more common *nōn*, we have no trace whatever of an intermediate form other than the dropping of final *-m*. I derive, then, Lat. *nōn* from **nō-n(e)*[2] as *quīn* from **quī-n(e)*, and *nōlo* from **nō-volo* as *prōrsus* from *prō-vorsus*.

The evidence for an I.E. form *nō* may be summarized here. Representatives of I.E. *noi* are, of course, evidence of the existence of an I.E. *nō*. The words which, as I believe, must be explained as containing I.E. *nō* are Lat. *nōn* and *nōlō* just discussed, Umbr. *no-sve*, O.Ir. *nā*. Either I.E. *nō* or *nē* or both may be seen in Aryan *nā* and its compounds. Forms to be explained as containing I.E. *noi* are Lat. (Duenos) *noi-si*, Lat. *noenum*, Lith. *nai-kaũ* and *nai-kinù*. Either I.E. *noi* or *nei* may be seen in Av. *naē-cis naē-da*, O.P. *naiy*, O.B. *ni*. Leaving out of account, then, Aryan, which furnishes as much evidence for the *no* forms as for the *ne*, and Arm., Gr., and Alb., which furnish no evidence for either, we have evidence for I.E. *nō* in Italic, Celtic, and Balto-Slavic, while for I.E. *nē* we have evidence in Italic, Celtic, Germanic, and Balto-Slavic.

Lat. *nei nī*, I.E. *nei*.

Besides the independent *nei nī* the word appears in *nīmīrum*, but not as a negative prefix. The word is an "elliptic paratactic protasis ' *non est mīrum.* ' "[3]

Lat. *noi* (in *noe-num* and *noi-si* (Duenos)), I.E. *noi*.

The common derivation of *noenum noenu*[4] from *ne-oinom* can only be made by supposing an elision in *n(e)*; but if I am cor-

---

[1] Plautus probably wrote *noenum* in a good many places in which it has disappeared from the text. *Cf.* Habich, De neg. usu Plaut., 35; Wagner to Aul., 67; Brix to Mil., 653.

[2] The above is in practical agreement with the derivation of *nōn* given by Wharton (Ety. Lat.) and with the discussion of *nōn* and *noenum* by Thomas (Class. Review, 5, 378, 434; 6, 194). *Cf.* further Wackernagel, Gr. Akzent, 19, n.; Stolz, Hist. Gr., 130, and Brugmann, I.F., 6, 80. My discussion was written some two years ago and before Mr. Thomas' article had come under my notice.

[3] So O. Brugmann, Ni, 19, and I have explained *nefas* similarly.

[4] The forms *nēnum* and *nēnu* are doubtless editor etymologies.

rect above in regard to *numquam* and *nusquam*, such an elision in sentence combination is unsupported. If *noenum* is from I.E. *noi-*, the second element is to be connected with the pronominal stem *no-* or *nu-*, and in either case with Lat. *num*.[9]

Unless Duenos *noisi*[1] is simply a dialectic variation of *nei*, we have in the word another evidence of I.E. *noi* in Latin. Solmsen's[2] objection to the view that *noi* is an ablaut form of *nei*, on the ground that there is no support for the form in related languages, amounts to little, even if the fact were exactly so, if it can be shown that representatives of an I.E, *nō* existed.

The negative *haud* has been connected by Corssen and others with Skr. *ava* and the negative force derived from the prepositional.

The final *-d* after the diphthong is in itself peculiar. It can hardly be an original *d*. But if we take *haut*[3] as the more original form, it is easy to suppose that *haud* arose by assimilation, after the law of the dropping of final *-d* had ceased to work, and that then *-d* was retained in certain sentence combinations and dropped in others (before consonants - *cf. sē-ponō* from *sēd-ponō*). The *h-* may not be etymological, and, rejecting this, we arrive at a form *aut* identical with the conjunction *au-t*,[4] "or." The original meaning of the particle *au-t*, as indicated by Skr. *ŏ*, Gr. *aử*, Lat. *au-tem*, was "further," "again," and I see no great difficulty in supposing that this *aut* was used with a negative as intensive[5] (*non aut*, "not again," "not at all"), and that thence the negative idea became attached to the word.[6] The weak *h-* was retained permanently in the negative and dropped permanently in the conjunction.

[1] Per Persson, I.F., 2, 206.

[2] *Cf.* Conway, A.J.P., 10, 455. If Conway's reading of the Duenos inscription is the correct one, *noine* does not occur.

[3] Solmsen, Stud. zur Lat. Lautge., 87, and *cf.* Conway, A.J.P., 10, 455; Planta, 1, 152.

[4] Habich (De neg. usu Plaut., 13), following Ritschl, takes *haud* as the more original form. *Cf.* Stolz, Lat. Gr., 317.

[5] For connections see p. 16.

[6] The use of *autem* as an intensive, not, however, of a negative, occurs occasionally in Plautus; *cf.* Pseud., 305, Amph., 901.

[7] Wharton, Ety. Lat., supposes the *h-* to be unorganic and compares *autem*. I do not know how he would connect the meanings of the two words.

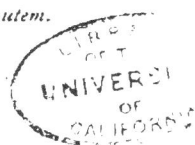

The origin of the negative meaning of *haud* is indicated by the collocation *neque . . . haud*, of which most of the examples are in Plautus. The examples are :[1]

Neque ego haud committam.   Bacch., 1037.

Neque id haud immerito tuo.   Men., 371.

Neque illud haud obiciet mihi.   Epid., 664.

Neque mihi haud imperito eveniet.   Persa, 535.

Neque id haud subditiva arbitror gloria esse.   Bacch., 26.

Neque haut longe post.   Gellius, 17, 21, 34.

Ne temere facias : neque tu haud dices tibi non praedictum.   Cave.
Ter. Andr., 205.[2]

It is to be noted that in the examples from Plautus and Terence *neque* and *haud* are separated by only one word, in that from Gellius not at all. The examples of *neque . . . numquam* differ in this respect, and, besides, such double negatives as *neque . . . nunquam* (negative and negative indefinite) are to be expected almost everywhere in literature and do not serve to explain *neque . . . haud.*[3] The nearness of the two negatives to each other would seem to preclude the supposition that the negatives were separated in their application, which is a necessary condition for the use of two negatives in the sense of one. If it were the case that the force of the *neque* was expended on the following word, *haud* would be left as the special negative of the verb in four of the seven cases, which is not the common use of this negative. It seems necessary, then, to separate *neque . . . haud* from such cases as Plautus, Curc., 579,[4] and Cato, R.R., 66.[5]

Neque . . . haud, except for the conjunction -*que*, is just like French *ne . . . pas*--the two are practically one word negativing the sentence.[6] We may conjecture that the few examples we have of the collocation are the survivals of a common form of expression. The dying out was the natural result of *haud* becoming an independent negative.

[1] *Cf.* Ziemer, Jung. Streif., 141 ; Habich, 7.

[2] Probably the true reading, although the MSS. have *hoc* in place of *haud*.

[3] *Cf.* Gebauer, Archiv f. Slav. Phil., 8, 177.

[4] *Ut ego tua magnifica verba, neque istas tuas magnas minas, non pluris facio quam ancillam meam.*

[5] See p. 6.

[6] The explanation given by Strong, Logeman, and Wheeler (Hist. of Lang., 155) of double negatives caused by contamination seems inapplicable here ; nor is it possible that *neque . . . haud* is a translation of a Gr. double negative.

It may well be that *haud* was allowed to stand by itself first in adjectival and adverbial expressions not closely connected with a verb and forming, as it were, an accentual unit. It is in such cases that French *ne pas* has become *pas* and *ne point point*. This would explain the common use of *haud* with adjectives and adverbs.

Lat. *in-* (as negative prefix), I.E. *n̥*.

OSCAN.

Osc. *nc*, I.E. *nc*.

Osc. *ni*, I.E. *nē*.

Osc. *nei*, I.E. *nei̯*.

All these Oscan negatives form compounds with *-p* (Lat. *-que*) the conjunction retaining its proper force.

Osc. *an-* (negative prefix), I.E. *n̥*.

UMBRIAN.

Umbr. *ne-* (in *ne-p*), I.E. *ne*.

Umbr. *nei-* (in *nei-p*), I.E. *nei̯*.

Umbr. *no-* (in *no-sve*), I.E. *nō*.

Umbr. *nosve* has usually been regarded as equal to Lat. *nisi*, though it was phonetically impossible to connect *no-* with Lat. *ni-, ni, ne,* or *nē*, and *nōn* seemed specifically Lat. So Brugmann[1] has proposed to see in the word not a negative, but a representative of I.E. *nu*, "now." But the supposition seems impossible for phonetic reasons.[2] I.E. *u* became *o* in Umbr. only under certain conditions, which will not include *nosve*. The usual representative was *u*, as shown by *fust, tuva,* etc.; while *u* became *o* only before *m*. The result before other *labials* was a " Mittellaut," which was sometimes written *u*, sometimes *o* (*sopa : supa*).

As for the meaning required for the word by the passage[3] in

---

[1] Osk. und Umbr., 225; *cf.* Bücheler, Umbrica, 96, and Breal, Eugubines, XXII.

[2] Von Planta, §§ 51-2.

[3] Ig. Tab. VI, B, 54. The passage with Breal's translation is as follows : . . . *cetu ehesu poplu. nosve ier che esu poplu, sopir habe esme pople, portatu ulo pue mersest, fetu uru pirse mers est:* "ito ex hoc populo. Si non iverit ex hoc populo, siquis incola est, huic populo [vectigal] portatu illuc ubi lex est, sacrificato id quod lex est."

which it occurs, it seems to me the negative is the more natural. It would seem that the object was to get rid of the "peregrini," and what they did after leaving the territory would be a matter of indifference to the Iguvini. The most natural thing after the decree of expulsion would be a threat against those who failed to obey that decree. *Habe*[1] is used absolutely, *i. e.*, with some word for "property" understood in thought, which word would then be supplied as the object of *portatu.* The sense would be then, "Let these people depart, but if they do not depart, whoever[2] has property shall contribute it for this people to be used in the coming sacrifice." If Brugmann's interpretation is the correct one, we should expect in place of *nosve*, "if now," *ponc*, "when," as he himself admits. Brugmann's interpretation apparently agrees better with the briefer direction in Table I;[3] but it may easily have been that "svepis habe, etc.," was understood as the penalty attached to the non-compliance with the sentence of banishment not here expressed.

Umbr. *an-* (as negative prefix), I.E. *n̥.*

OLD IRISH.

I.E. *mē* does not appear in Celtic. O.Ir. *mi-* (negative prefix) probably corresponds to Germanic *miss-*.[4]

O.Ir. *nī*, I.E. *nē.*

The negative is used with *con* and in the compound *ma-ni,* "if not."

O.Ir. *nā*, I.E. *nō.*

The word further appears in the compounds *nád, nách, arná, arnach, arnad, conna, connaro.*

Also in Scotch Gaelic and Welsh *nī* and *nā* appear as the representatives of I.E. *nē* and *nō* respectively.

O.Ir. *an-*,[5] *am-*, *e-* (negative prefix), I.E. *n̥.*

---

[1] *Cf.* Harper's Lex., *sub v. habeo*, II, A.

[2] *Sepir* = "quisquis;" Brugmann, Osk. und Umbr., 214, and v. Plauta, 152.

[3] Tab. I, *b*, 17, 18, eturstamu tuta . . . : "svepis habe, purtatulu, pue mers est, feitu usu, pere mers est," which Bücheler translates, "exterminato urbem . . . siquis habet, portato illo quo jus est, facito illo quod jus est."

[4] *Cf.* Kluge, *sub v. miss-*, and Feist, *sub v. miss-*.

[5] In regard to *an(a)-* *cf.* Zimmer, K.Z., 24, 532.

GOTHIC.

Goth. *ni*, I.E. *ne*.

Goth. *ni* appears further in the compounds *niba nibai, nih, niu*. The *-h*[1] of *nih* is the I.E. *qe*, Skr. *ca*, Gr. *τε*, Lat. *-que*, Osc.-Umbr. *-p*.   Goth. *niu*[2] (interrogative) contains the enclitic particle *u* (Vedic *u*, etc.) and so would correspond in form almost exactly with Lat. *neu* ($<ne\text{-}u$), though the composition in the two lan-guages was doubtless independent.

Goth. *nē*, I.E. *nē*.

Goth. *nei*, I.E. *nei̯*.

OLD HIGH GERMAN.

O.H.G. *ni*, I.E. *ne*.

O.H.G. *niwiht, niowiht, nein, nio, nioman*, etc., show *ni* com-pounded with various pronominal words. O.H.G. *noh*, "neither," can hardly be explained as phonetically from I.E. *ne + qe*—the form should correspond with Goth. *nih*. Paul's[3] and Braune's[4] supposition of a change of *e* to *o* in enclitics and proclitics seems uncertain and perhaps would not apply here if established. One might see here I.E. *nō*. But more probably the similarity of form of *noh* (Goth. *nauh*, I.E. *nu-qe*) and the use of that particle as an intensive to a negative caused it to assume the force of *nih*, driv-ing that particle out of use as an independent adverb and thence influencing the vowel in the compound *nih(h)ein (noh(h)ein : nih-(h)ein*.[5])

[1] *Cf.* Sonne, K.Z., 12, 279; Dahlmann, J.P., 2, 257 ; Brugmann, II, 411 ; Scherer, Z.G.D.S., 476. Scherer would connect Goth. *-h* with Lat. *-c*, Gr. *-κ* in *οὐκ(ί)*

[2] *Cf.* Scherer, Sonne, and Dahlmann as above, and J. Schmidt, Vocalismus, I, 152.

[3] P.B.B., 6, 248.

[4] Ahd. Gr., § 29.

[5] The usual derivation of *nihhein* from *nih ein* seems hardly satisfactory. *Nihhein* and *dehhein* must be considered together. If the latter is from a *deh + ein* (*cf.* Kluge, *sub v. kein*), there is no explanation for **deh-*. The occurrence of *-hh-* (beside *-h-*) in both words might not be difficult of explana-tion (*cf.* Braune, A.H.G. Gr., § 154, A, 6), but *nih* with meaning "and not" could hardly enter the compound, and we have no evidence of the uncom-pounded adverb meaning simply "not." It is difficult to understand under what circumstances *dechein* became *kein* in M.H.G. Would it not be better to suppose that the first member of the compound *dehein* is the article as in *de-*

NORTH GERMANIC.

In North Germanic all I.E. negative adverbs disappeared. Besides the negative verbal suffix *-at*, which Noreen[1] connects with Goth. *ainata*, a negative appears in the various dialects, *e. g.*, O.Ic. *ekke*, compounded of *eit*, neuter of *ein*, and a particle *-ge*, *-gi*. This particle[2] is the same one that appears in *man(n)-ge*, "Niemand," *hver-ge*, "nirgends," and so is plainly responsible for the negative force of *ek-ke*, etc.

Germanic *un-*[3] (negative prefix), I.E. *n*.

O.H.G. *ā-*, O.E. *ǣ-* (negative prefix), I.E. *n̄-* (?).

In O.H.G. some ten or fifteen[4] words appear with this prefix, among which are *ā-teil*, "non-participation," and *ā-māht*, whence the N.H.G. *Ohnmacht* (dialectic *Oh-macht*), with *-n* from the commoner prefix *un-*.[5] The number of examples could be added to from M.H.G. In O.E. some ten or twelve words have *ǣ* as negative prefix, *e. g.*, *ǣ-men*, "unmanned," *ǣ-not*, "useless." If now these prefixes are to be connected, as it seems they should be, they point to an urgermanic vowel sound differing but little, if any, in degree of *openness* from urgermanic *ē*. But *ę̄*,[6] as a negative prefix would stand entirely by itself, unless it is to be connected with I.E. *n̄*.

---

weder? (This can hardly be for **deh-weder*, as Braune would have it — § 295, A, 2; *cf. ni weder*.) If the compound were formed early, *-hh-* would be regularly for Germanic *-k-*, and *-h-* would be a simplification seen in other cases. We would have, then, for the last member a Germanic pronoun *kein*, and in the case of *nihhein* the first member would be *ni-*, as in *ni weder*. This *kein*, or at least its initial, is to be connected in some way with the *-k* of Goth. *mi-k*, *thu-k*, *si-k*, which may be identified with the Gr. γε. Compare also Skr. *ha*, *gha*, and *-g* of Lat. *neg*. (*Cf.* Curtius, Grundzüge, 526; and Havet, Mem. Soc. Ling., 6, 118.)

[1] Altic. und Altnorw. Gr., § 57, 4 *b*.

[2] Noreen, 71, and *cf.* above, p. 7.

[3] On O.H.G. *una-* in *una-holda*, see p. 8.

[4] *Cf.* Weinhold, M.H.G. Gr., § 291, who connects O.H.G. *ā-*, with Skr. *a-*. Grimm, 695, connects O.H.G. *ā-* with the preposition, Goth. *us*, etc.

[5] Andresen, Deutsche Volksetymologie, 275.

[6] *ę̄* represents the sound just mentioned and which, as I shall try to show, was a more or less nasalized vowel sound slightly more closed than urgermanic *ē*.

It is to be noted that in all the O:H.G. and O.E. words the prefix appears before a consonant. It might well be that an ante-vocalic form of the prefix was displaced by the common *un-*. So we are at liberty to suppose for the urgermanic sound some sort of nasal affection (nasalization, glide sound, or both), which should disappear in O.H.G. before consonants, but which might be found to appear before vowels.

The O.H.G., Goth., and Gr. words for "without" — *ānu, inu,* and *ἄνευ* — are of value in the discussion. Kluge[1] and others have connected these words, but I do not think the phonetics have been made clear. If we suppose, now, that the urgermanic sound mentioned above was *slightly closer* than urgermanic *ē̆*, there is no difficulty in supposing as representatives of it Goth. *in-*, O.H.G. *ān-*, before vowels, and O.H.G. *ā-*, O.E. *ā̄-*, before consonants. This will permit us to connect directly Goth. *inu* and O.H.G. *anu āno āna,* O.S. *ano,* O.Ic. *ōn ān.* They are representatives of I.E. *n̄n-u.*

Gr. *ἄνευ* has been connected with Skr. *sanutar.*[2] To say nothing of the initial smooth breathing, the identity in meaning and the apparent resemblance in form of Gr. *ἄνευ* and O.H.G. *ānu,* Goth. *inu,*[3] should lead us to suppose that *ἄνευ* was connected, not with *sanutar,*[4] but with the Germanic words. This can be done by supposing beside I.E. *n̄n-u* a form *n̄n-eu.* The last element in these forms is the particle *u,* Vedic *u,* etc., and the first, as I think, the I.E. *u ū,* which appears in the separate languages as a negative prefix.[5]

[1] Kluge, *s. v. ohne;* Feist, *sub v. inu;* Prellwitz, *sub v. ἄνευ*; Bezzenberger, Adverb., 84; Noreen. Urgermanische Lautlehre, 85. Noreen connects the words with the various forms of the negative *ne,* but in a way hardly satisfactory, it seems to me.

[2] Bartholomae, B.B., 15, 16, and *cf.* Meringer, B.B., 16, 227, and Johansson, B.B., 15, 310.

[3] O.B. *vūnŭ* is doubtless for *vĭnŭ,*—*cf. vĭne* Skr. *vinā*; *cf.* Jagic Archiv. f. slav. Phil. 1, 17, Per Persson, I.F., 2, 213 and references. Possibly also a Skr. *ano* is to be added; see B. and R., *sub v.* For the Ossetan *änä* see Hübsch-mann, Oss. Sprache, 21.

[4] With Skr. *sanutar sanitur* are connected Gr. *ἄτερ* and *ἀτάρ,* the aspiration being lost through the influence of *ἄνευ* and *αὖταρ* (Brugmann, II, 75). Gr. *ἄνις* from *ἄνευ* after χωρίς (Brugmann, Gr. Gr., 218).

[5] This derivation of Goth. *inu,* O.H.G. *ānu,* Gr. *ἄνευ,* as well as that of the O.H.G. *ā-*, O.E. *ǣ* , is in conflict with the theory advanced by Fierlinger (K.Z.,

There may be difficulty in supposing that a compound adverb-preposition *ṇn-eu* was formed from *ṇ*, which regularly appears as a negative prefix, and a particle *u*.   However, remembering that originally *ṇ* was an independent word negativing a noun and, that so, it could have a particle as *u* attached to it, and remembering that *ṇ-eḱṇos* came to mean "without a horse," we may be allowed to conjecture that *ṇ eu eḱṇos* came to have the same meaning, although the words did not form so close a compound that *ṇn-eu* would be unable to be separated as an adverb-preposition meaning "without."[1]   Something very near the reverse of this process is to be seen, for example, in Skr. *nirmakṣikam*, "with freedom from flies."

LITHUANIAN.

Lith. *nè*, I.E. *ne.*

The use of the particle was extended and drove out entirely the representatives of I.E. *ṇ-* and *ṇ̄-* as negative prefixes.   It did *not* form negative indefinite pronouns and adverbs.   It was strengthened by particles *-gi* and *-gu*, and formed a conjunctional compound *neba* (*cf.* the Av. particle *bā*).

27, 436, and *cf.* Kluge, *sub v.*, Art., and Wood, Red. Verbs in Germ., 34) that the Germanic representation of I.E. *ṇ̄* was *an*.   But the only apparent support for this theory is furnished by Germanic *gaggan* and *blandan*, which have congeners with an *-e-* form of root, and O.E. *and* (Kluge, P.B.B., 10, 444).   The analogy of the long sonant liquids will give no support here, since the representations of sonant liquids and sonant nasals in the separate developments differ as often as they agree.   *Cf.* further Hübschmann, Vocalismus, 134 f.; Brugmann, I, 306 : Osthoff, Perfect., 178, 417 ; and de Saussure, System Prim., 274.   De Saussure supposes that the Goth. representation of *ṇ̄* was *un*, and so also Streitberg, I.F., 6, 141.   I am not unaware of the narrow basis upon which my own theory rests, but, on the other hand, I believe nothing very definite can be urged against it.   To be sure, *n* is not assumed to have existed before vowels, as I have supposed in the case of the I.E. *ṇ̄n-n* : Goth. *inn*, O.H.G. *ânu*.   But even if the rule were definitely established, it could not be applied with certainty to a case of this kind.   The *-n* may have become attached to the *ṇ̄* in a late period of the I.E., when the accentual laws which had caused the differentiation of *ṇ* and *ṇ̄* had ceased to work.   It is possible that I.E. *ṇ̄-* (negative prefix) occurs in Goth. *in-winds*, "unjust," and *inwidan*, "to refuse to recognize," and I.E. *ṇ* in *sinteins, sinteino,* "πάντοτε."   (For the suffix, compare Lat. *mātūtīnus, diūtinus, perendinus;* but see Brugmann, Die Ausdrücke für den Begriff der Totalität, 23.)

[1] Delbrück, Ver. Syntax, 299, gives Gr. *ἄνευ*, Goth. *inuh*, as an example of prepositions which were proethnic and which were not præverbia.

Lith. *neì* (*në-*), I.E. *neị*.

In contrast with *ne neì* was not used as a true negative prefix and *did* form indefinite pronouns and adverbs, *e. g.*, *neî venas*, "no one" (beside *nevëns*, "not one," "many").

Lith. *nai-*, I.E. *noị*.

The word only occurs in *naikaũ* and the more common *nai-kinù*, "tilgen." Beside *naikinù* we have *nëkinù*, "verachten," the latter evidently being a denominative of *nëkas*. We must suppose that there once existed in Lith. the indefinite pronouns *nai-kas* and *neị-kas*, from each of which a denominative was formed.[1]

.

OLD BULGARIAN.

O.B. *ne*, I.E. *ne*.

O.B. *ni*, I.E. *neị* or *noị*.

As in the case of the corresponding words in Lith., O.B. *ne* is used as a negative prefix and *ni* to form negative indefinites.

SYNTAX.[2]

None of the negatives of separate origin was prohibitive,[3] *i. e.*, used with volitive forms. Negative prefixes sometimes arose, practically equivalent to the representatives of I.E. u or $\bar{u}$, *e. g.*, Lith. *be-*, O.B. *bez-*.

Of the representatives of the I.E. forms, *ne në no nõ neị noị*, *më*, the syntactical uses as they appear in the various languages may be classified as 1) prohibitive, 2) convictional, 3) conjunctional, 4) negative of dependent sentences, 5) conditional, 6) interrogative.

[1] The relation of *nykstù* to *nëkinu* and *naikinu* I do not attempt to discuss. It may be an afformate to these words, or may be entirely distinct and to be connected with *ninkù nikañ*, Lett. *nikus*, O.B. *niknǫti*. *Cf.* J. Schmidt, Plural-bildung, 396, n., and Leskien, Der Ablaut der Wurzelsilben im Lith., 279.

[2] It is proposed here to discuss briefly the syntactical uses of the negatives of the various languages, mainly with the view of discovering the original value of the I.E. negatives and the relations existing between that original value and the values attached to the negatives of the separate languages.

[3] Sacrificing exactness to convenience I use the term "*prohibitive*" as indicated, "*volitive forms*" for forms expressing *will* or *wish*, "convictional negative" as opposed to "prohibitive," *i. e.*, the negative of expressions of conviction, expectation, possibility, etc. On Goth. *ibai* and O.B. *jeda*, see p. 14, n.

The last two[1] can only be regarded as specializations in the use of the convictional or prohibitive negatives. A special negative for dependent sentences is found, I believe, only in Celtic, and there the distinction was not always kept up. The use of Celtic *nā* in dependent sentences is probably connected with its use with volitive forms.

The conjunctional use of a negative is only to be seen — with certainty[2] at least — in the case of Skr. *nēd*, Gr. μή, Lat. *nē*, and O.H.G. *ni*. In all these cases, except that of Skr. *nēd*, it is easy to see that the conjunctional force arose through the development of the clause introduced by it from an independent through a paratactic to hypotactic clause of purpose, etc. But the case of Skr. *nēd* is somewhat different. In independent sentences there was no distinction between *na* and *nēd*,[3] and neither was to any great extent the negative of the subjunctive with its volitive force. The ordinary paratactic expression of purpose was with *mā* and the injunctive.[4] But we may suppose that beside the paratactic *mā* with injunctive or even, perhaps, earlier than that construction for purpose, there was a paratactic expression of purpose with *nēd* (and *na*) with the subjunctive, not descended directly from an expression of negative will, but formed by adding a negative to the positive expression legitimately using the subjunctive.[5] It might well be that *nēd* should be introduced into and become the generally used negative in these sentences without being freely used in expressions of a more evident volitive character.

The facts indicate that the conjunctional use of the negative

[1] The last is altogether uncertain. The only case is Goth. *nei*, and that occurs with interrogative force without an interrogative word but once. Lat. *nei nī* and Osc. *ne* are the only examples of a conditionally used negative. For *nī*, see O. Brugmann, Nī. Osc. *ne* only once and that with *pún,—ne pún.* "nisi cum."

[2] I venture the opinion that the sentences introduced by *mā* in the Av. should not be considered as dependent. The fact that *ma* was not so used in Skr., O.P., or in the modern Persian and the possibility of considering the examples paratactic should lead one to that view.

[3] Delbrück, Syn. Forsch., I, 112, 121 ; Whitney, J.A.O.S., 5, 385, 399.

[4] Delbrück, Syn. Forsch., V, 546.

[5] Beside the subjunctive and equivalent to it in these clauses is, of course, the injunctive, and the optative occurs once (A.B., 8,'23, 11).

did not belong to the parent speech.[1] The use does not appear in near all these languages; the negatives so used are not the same in any two of them, the negative so used in Skr. is a special Aryan strengthened form of I.E. *ne;* only the purpose clause appears in Skr., while in the other languages also substantive clauses are so introduced; the conjunctional use of O.H.G.[2] *ni* is quite certainly a special development, since the use does not appear in Gothic.

We have left, then, two values possible for the I.E. negatives — prohibitive and convictional.

The value of I.E. *mē* was either that of a prohibitive negative or one from which such a value could be derived. In all languages in which it occurs it has a more or less restricted prohibitive value.

On the other hand, for the representatives of I.E. *ne* and its ablaut forms, with the exception of *n ñ*, the separate languages show variations. The form *ne* never became a special prohibitive. In Germanic and Balto-Slavic, where no distinction was made, I.E. *ne*[3] was used as convictional and prohibitive; and in Skr., while *na* was sometimes used with volitive forms, *mā* was peculiarly the prohibitive negative. The form *nē* became specially prohibitive only in Latin, but the convictional value is retained in the collocation *nē . . . quidem.* The form *nei* was also used in Latin as a prohibitive, but it never became restricted to this use. The form *nō* became prohibitive only in Celtic, and there I.E. *nē* was not altogether excluded from use with imperative and subjunctive. The use of O.Ir. *mā* in dependent sentences is possibly connected with its use as a prohibitive. It is noteworthy

---

[1] This would furnish some evidence in support of the statement that the parent speech did not possess dependent sentences. *Cf.* Hermann, K.Z., 23, 481 f.; Zimmer, Festgruss an Roth, 173. If negative purpose clauses are not proethnic, probably positive purpose clauses are not. Probably also all sentences introduced by a *sentence* relative (*i. e.*, relative adverb) are to be classed as not proethnic. Further than this, however, the evidence furnished by the absence of conjunctionally used negatives would not reach.

[2] O.H.G. *ni*, "dass nicht," "quin," only after negative sentences.

[3] In Latin probably the use of *ne* as a prohibitive survives in a few cases of *neque (nec)* with volitive subjunctive, *e. g.*, Plautus, Asin., 775 ff. (*cf.* Elmer, A. J.P., 15, 299 ff., especially 319; Loch, Imperativus bei Plautus; and A.J.P., 16, No. 4). In Oscan *nep* (Lat. *nec*) was used with volitive forms, and in Umbrian *nep* is used with an imperative (*neip . . . nep*, VI, A, 6).

that, while in Latin *nē* was prohibitive, *nō-n* (*e*) convictional, in O.Ir., so far as the distinction was made, *nā* (Lat. *nō-*) was prohibitive and *nī* (Lat. *nē*) convictional.   The form *noi* nowhere shows signs of being a prohibitive.

We shall be safe in saying that originally none of these forms of *ne* had a *special* prohibitive force, and that the development or specialization took place in each instance to meet a want for some reason not felt in the I.E. period.

What, now, was the relation of *mē* to *ne* and its ablaut forms? The persistent use of *mē* as a more or less restricted prohibitive wherever it occurs precludes the supposition that *mē* and *ne* were used indiscriminately.   And it is about equally certain that *mē* and *ne* were not contrasted as the negatives of volitive and non-volitive forms respectively.   If such a distinction had been established in I.E. times, we should expect to find it more generally kept up, and especially in all those languages in which the distinction of prohibitive and convictional negatives appear we should expect to find *mē* retained.   In Italic and Celtic, however, we have the distinction of prohibitive and convictional negative, but *mē* has disappeared.   Whether, now, we suppose that in Latin *mē* died out before *nē* became prohibitive, or that *nē* became prohibitive and displaced *mē*, we should be obliged to suppose that the distinction died out and arose anew, and this is not probable.   But the strongest argument against supposing that *mē* bore the same relation to *ne* in I.E. that μή did to οὐ in Gr. is furnished by the state of affairs we find in Skr., supplemented by that in Av., O.P., and Gr.   The most important fact is that in Vedic Skr. *mā*[1] is used only with the injunctive.   So far as we can judge, the older Avestan[2] was the same as the older Skr.; the Gathas have *mā* only with the injunctive.   In O.P. *mā* generally has the injunctive, sometimes the optative.   In Gr. the use of μή with the *aorist* subjunctive, contrasted with the use of the same particle with present imperative, would seem to be a continuation[3] of the use of the negative with the aorist injunctive, which Avery's[4]

[1] Grassmann, *sub v. ma;* Delbrück, Syn. Forsch., V, 358.   The only exception of importance, if not absolutely, is the use of *ma* with the optative *bhujēma*, which itself does not occur without *ma*.

[2] Spiegel, Alter. Gr., 520.

[3] *Cf.* C. W. E. Miller, A.J.P., 418 f., and Delbrück, Syn. Forsch., V, 358.

[4] J.A.O S., 13, 326 f.

statistics show to have been the most common tense, especially in the earliest Sanskrit. Possibly, too, the more energetic character of the perfect in prohibitions in Latin and the preference for the perfect after the negative in Oscan is to be brought into this connection.[1]

Now it can hardly be that *mā* (I.E. *mē̆*) was originally used freely with volitive forms and later was restricted to use with the injunctive, for, even in Skr., the injunctive was the least distinctively volitive of all the volitive forms and probably at a period not much antedating the Rig Veda was not modal at all.[2] The conclusion is, then, that *mē̆* in I.E. was, in a way, prohibitive, but used only with the injunctive or, in other words, that the proethnic method of expressing prohibition and negative wish was by means of *mē̆* and the injunctive.[3] This conclusion is supported by the fact that in Vedic Skr. the imperative has no negative and by the restricted use of the negative with the imperative in Latin. The true original force of *mē̆* appears when we consider the probable original value of the injunctive. If the injunctive was non-modal,[4] *i. e.*, did not express *will* or *wish*, then it is plain that in a collocation of *mē̆* and injunctive expressing negative will or wish the modal idea must have been expressed by the *mē̆*, and only the verbal idea was conveyed by the injunctive. So *don't* in English is strictly speaking not the negative of a following verb, and there may be no conscious connection with the negative *not*, but it is an expression of prohibition or negative will to which various verbal ideas may be added by means of the colorless infinitive. Indeed, instead of believing that *mē̆* was originally a negative of a modal form, we may rather conjecture that the modal force of the injunctive proceeded from this very use with *mē̆* in prohibition, or, at least, that the development of modal force was thus greatly assisted. In the collocation of *mē̆* and injunctive *mē̆* was *negative volitive*, the injunctive verbal, later *mē̆* was felt as negative and the injunctive as *volitive verbal*.

[1] *Cf.* Buck, Verb-system, 140; Elmer, A.J.P., 15, 115 f.

[2] Note the increasing modality of the injunctive, as shown by Avery's statistics. The ratio of non-modal to modal cases in R.V. is 1:1, in A.V. 1:10. *Cf.* Thurneysen, K.Z., 27, 172 f.; Brugmann, M.U., 3, 1, f., and Grundriss, II, 414.

[3] Delbrück, Syn. Forsch., IV, 147.

[4] *Cf.* Thurneysen as above.

So long as the original feeling was kept up, as in Vedic Skr., *mā* (*mḗ*) could not be extended to other volitive forms. But we are not surprised to note that those other volitive forms sometimes took the negative used with non-volitive forms. So *na* was used with subjunctive, optative, and even with the injunctive, but never with imperative. But later in Skr., when *mā́* was felt as a true negative, its use could be and was extended to other volitive forms ;[1] and the same thing took place in Later Av., O.P., Arm., Gr., and Alb. On the other hand, in Germanic and Balto-Slavic the process, begun in Vedic Skr., of extending the use of *ne* to volitive forms was consistently carried out, and the expression of prohibition thus produced drove out the older *mḗ* with injunctive. In Italic and Celtic, in the same way, the convictional negatives came to be used with volitive forms, and the old form of prohibition died out. Further, in these languages one or another ablaut form was specialized and became with more or less consistency the special negative of volitive forms.

[1] To imperative, optative, future, infinitive, and gerund. *Cf.* Speijer, § 353, 4. The use of *mā́* with augmented past forms was an extension of the modal force of the injunctive rather than an extension of the use of *mā́*.

www.ingramcontent.com/pod-product-compliance
Lightning Source LLC
Chambersburg PA
CBHW032139080426
42733CB00008B/1133